AF505812

Amy Patton

Blaffer Art Museum

Published on the occasion of the exhibition *Amy Patton* held at Blaffer Art Museum, August 28–November 13, 2010. The exhibition and publication are made possible in part by the Cecil Amelia Blaffer von Furstenberg Endowment for Exhibitions and Programs, Centex Beverage Inc., and Houston Endowment Inc. In-kind support is provided by Continental Airlines. Amy Patton was the University of Houston Cynthia Woods Mitchell Center for the Arts Spring 2010 Artist-in-Residence. Additional residency support was provided by Blaffer Art Museum and School of Theatre & Dance at the University of Houston.

Blaffer Art Museum
University of Houston
120 Fine Arts Building
Houston, Texas 77204–4018
www.blafferartmuseum.org

©2010 Blaffer Art Museum. All rights reserved. No part of this book may be reproduced in any form or by any electronic or mechanical means, including information storage or retrieval systems, without permission in writing from the publishers, except by a reviewer who may quote brief passages in a review.

Design: Narrow Gauge
Editor: Lucy Flint
Printer: Lulu Enterprises, Inc.

U.S. Distributor:
D.A.P./Distributed Art Publishers, Inc.
155 Sixth Avenue, 2nd Floor
New York, New York 10013
Tel: 212 627 1999
Fax: 212 627 9484
www.artbook.com

New Zealand Distributor:
Narrow Gauge
narrowgauge@splitfountain.org

All images are courtesy of the artist unless otherwise noted.
Courtesy NASA/JPL-Caltech:
1–3, 16–17, 32–33, 100–104
Photography dabfoto creative:
5–9, 31, 34–38, 82–83, 90–93
Photography James Duncan Davidson:
48–49, 64–65, 74–75, 80–81, 88–89

Library of Congress
Cataloging-in-Publication Data

Hooper, Rachel, 1980–
Amy Patton : bitter, black thoughts /
Rachel Hooper; with contributions by
Christina Linden and Ingo Niermann.
p. cm.
"Published on the occasion of the
exhibition Amy Patton, held at
Blaffer Art Museum, August
28–November 13, 2010."
Includes bibliographical references.

ISBN 978-0-941193-48-1

1. Patton, Amy, 1979—Exhibitions.
2. Patton, Amy, 1979—Interviews.
3. Experimental films—Exhibitions.
I. Patton, Amy, 1979–
II. Blaffer Art Museum at the University of Houston.
III. Title.
N6537.P29A4 2010
700.92–dc22
2010029525

BLAFFER

CONTENTS

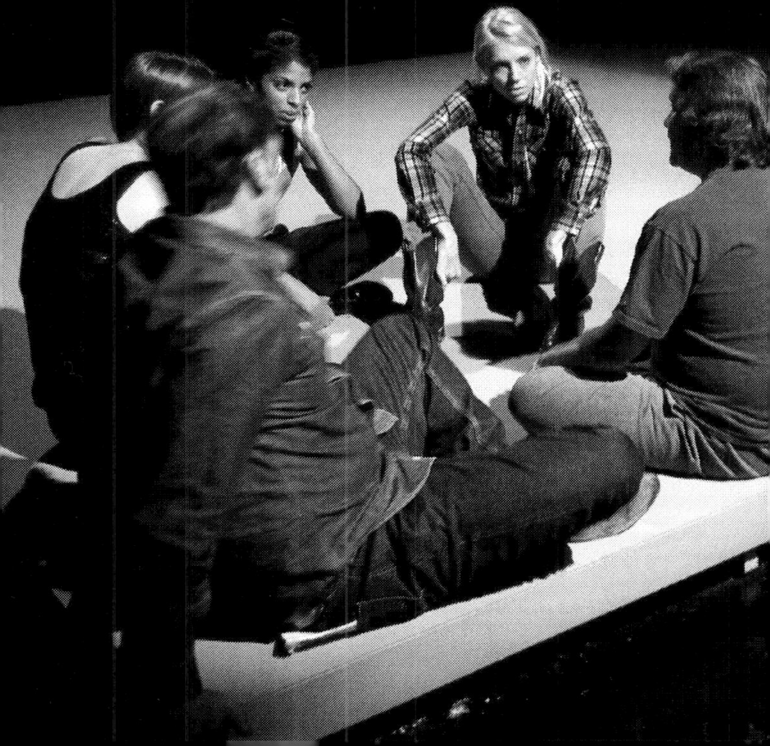

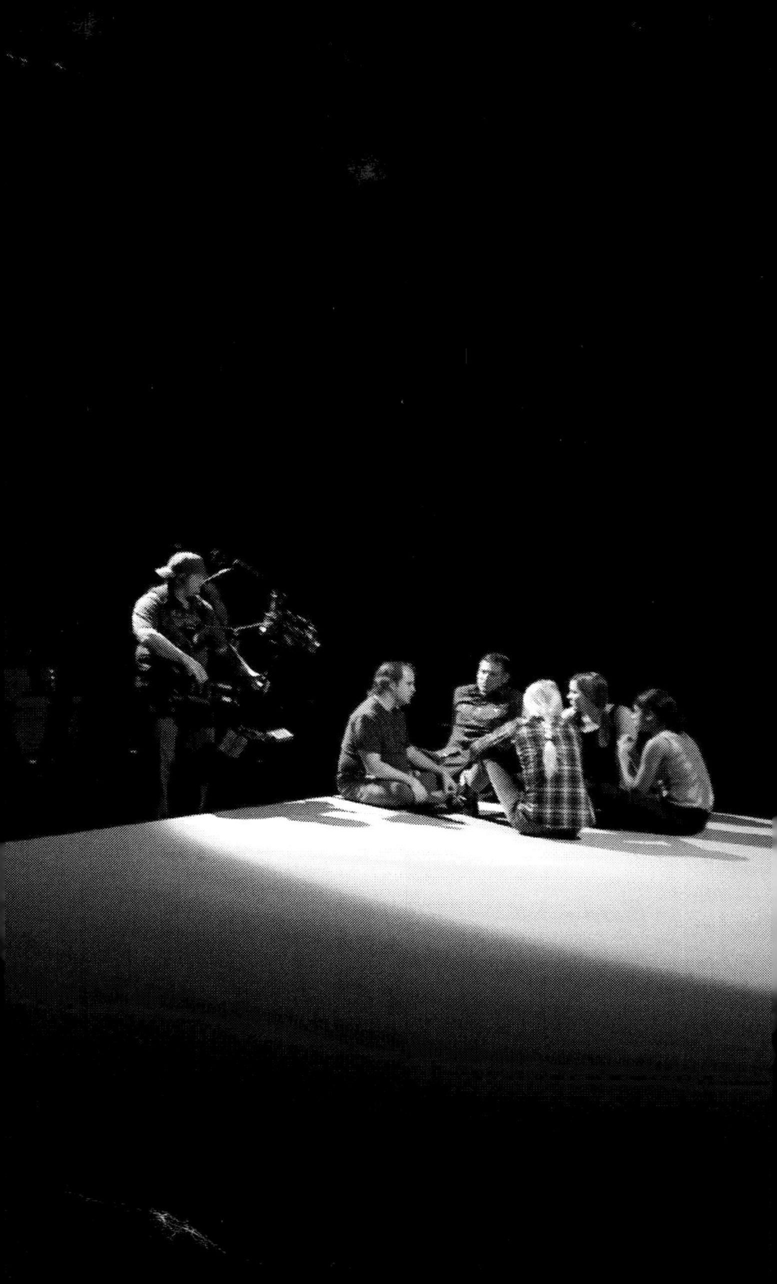

DIRECTOR'S PREFACE

Amy Patton's exhibition at Blaffer Art Museum at
the University of Houston is the result of a yearlong
collaboration between the museum, the artist, the
University of Houston's Cynthia Woods Mitchell
Center for the Arts, and the UH School of Theatre
& Dance.

The centerpiece of the exhibition, *Oil*, is both a
filmed theater piece and a documentary on the making
of the film itself. Made in and for Houston, it takes
Upton Sinclair's novel by the same title as a point of
departure for an open performative engagement with
the generative engine of this city's economy. During
a four-week residency made possible by the Mitchell
Center for the Arts, the artist involved a group of
highly talented theater students as well as some of
this city's finest professional actors in actively shaping
and defining the script and direction of the film.

Predating the recent oil spill in the Gulf of Mexico
and the ensuing crisis of epic proportion, Patton's choice
of theme was motivated by her desire to tap into
associations commonly made with Houston in order to
loosely situate her experiment with filmic construction
and narrative. In the wake of the catastrophic events
surrounding the explosion on Deepwater Horizon, the
project takes on an uncanny timeliness in positing the
defining character of our society's reliance on natural
energy resources at the center of artistic agency.

I thank Rachel Hooper, associate curator at Blaffer
and Mitchell Center Curatorial Fellow, for bringing
Amy Patton's work to my attention and conceiving of
a compelling installation of this newly commissioned

piece alongside existing works. I am grateful to Karen
Farber, director of the Mitchell Center and special
assistant to the provost and community liaison for
UH Arts, and Steven W. Wallace, director of the
University of Houston School of Theatre & Dance,
as well as their staff, for their enthusiastic support of
the residency. As always, the entire Blaffer staff needs
to be acknowledged for their incessant efforts toward
realizing the museum's artistic and curatorial vision.

This project could not have been realized without
the aid of our funders Centex Beverage, Inc., Continental
Airlines, and Houston Endowment, Inc. I would like
to thank them for their generous support of Blaffer's
exhibitions and programs. Additional support
came from The Cecil Amelia Blaffer von Furstenberg
Endowment for Exhibitions and Programs.

My final thanks go to Amy Patton for enriching
Blaffer's programs with this exhibition. We are proud
to be the first museum to present a significant body of
work previously unseen in the United States.

Claudia Schmuckli

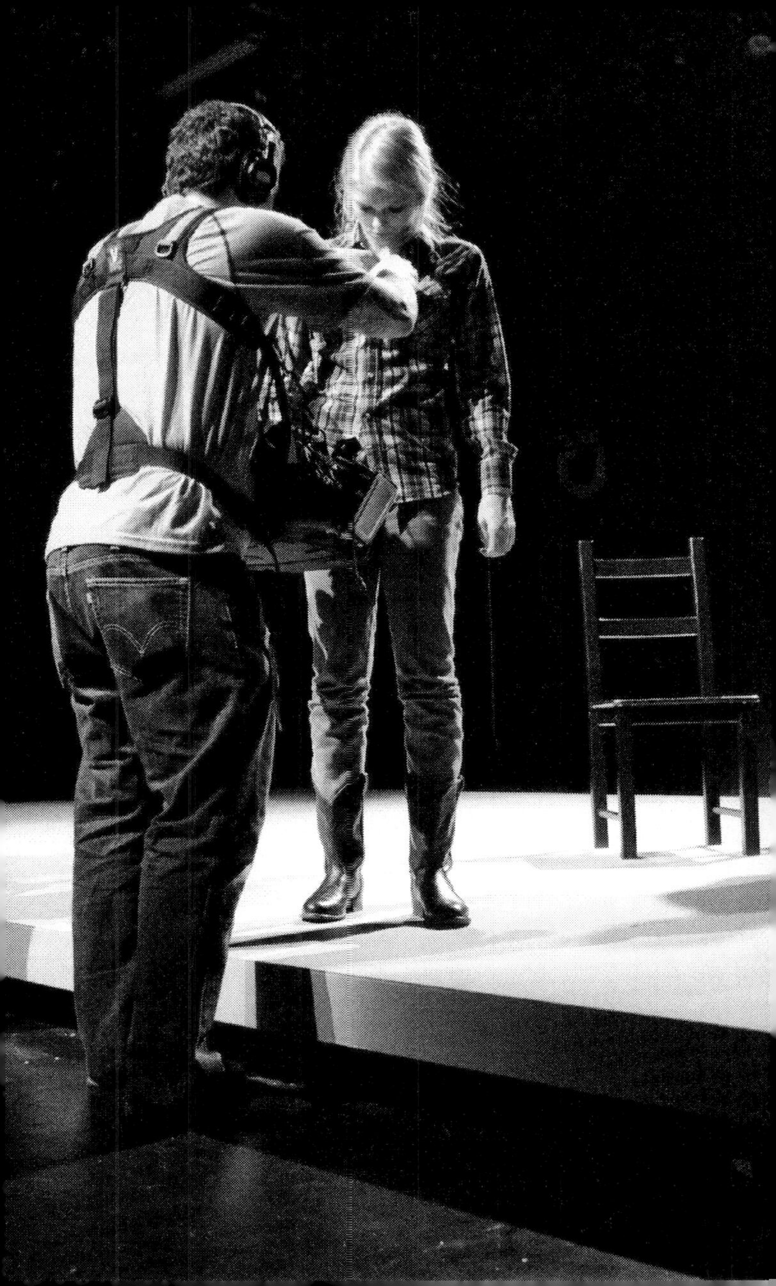

CURATOR'S ACKNOWLEDGMENTS

It has been a joy to work with Amy on all aspects of
her Blaffer project as it grew beyond an exhibition to
also comprise a residency, a commissioned film, and a
catalogue. Her work has shown me a new way of thinking
about narrative and voiceovers in the context of experimental film, and I am delighted that she so imaginatively
embraced the multifaceted project. On behalf of everyone
who has worked with her at Blaffer and the university,
I would like to thank Amy for her openness to collaboration, for allowing us to share in her process and giving
each of us the freedom to be a creative partner.

Amy's ideas were realized through the efforts of
many people. Blaffer staff and interns Jasmine Moses,
Samantha Jarvis, Catherine Krause, and Joe Gracely have
provided crucial support, and their intelligence and
creativity have enhanced the exhibition in countless
ways. Karen Farber and Steven W. Wallace invited Amy
to come to the University of Houston for a residency
and commissioned the film that is the centerpiece of her
exhibition at Blaffer. I am grateful for their leadership
and the important contributions made by the staff and
faculty of the Mitchell Center and the School of Theatre
& Dance. My warm thanks also go to Terrie Sultan,
former director of Blaffer and current director of the
Parrish Art Museum, for first believing in the potential
of this project and encouraging me to pursue it. I also
want to thank Aurora Picture Show for hosting an
artist's talk by Amy during her residency.

UH Theatre instructor and Alley Company member
Justin Doran helped Amy put together the terrific cast
for the film—Katt Gilcrease, Mia Pipkin, David R.

Rainey, Tracie Thomason, Danielle Bunch, and Chris Viles. Amy and I are grateful to Nathan Haworth, who was an invaluable technical wiz, helping with everything from lighting to set design, and Anthony Contello, who saved the day with his stage construction. The work of director of photography Lisa Rave was outstanding, and she collaborated effectively with the good folks at South Coast Video, Adam Risner at Szabo Sound, and Scott Budge at Real Time Pictures to ensure that the production went smoothly. Nancy Zastudil, founder of PLAND and former Mitchell Center associate director, deserves special recognition for managing all aspects of the residency with her usual grace and good humor. Thanks also go to Christian Obermeyer, who helped mix the sound in post-production, and Johan Møller Carlsen, who worked closely with Amy to craft a montage for *Oil*.

My sincere thanks go to Christina Linden and Ingo Niermann for their thoughtful contributions to this catalogue. Layla Tweedie-Cullen of Narrow Gauge worked closely with Amy to create a beautiful book, deftly capturing the spirit of Amy's work in her design. David Brown at dabfoto creative took the gorgeous production shots that appear throughout the book. As editor, the gifted Lucy Flint has been wonderful to work with during this period when we are revising our publication standards along with the redesign of Blaffer's identity.

I am deeply grateful to Blaffer director and chief curator Claudia Schmuckli for giving Amy and me her complete trust and support. Her guidance and vision have been essential in making this project a success.

Rachel Hooper

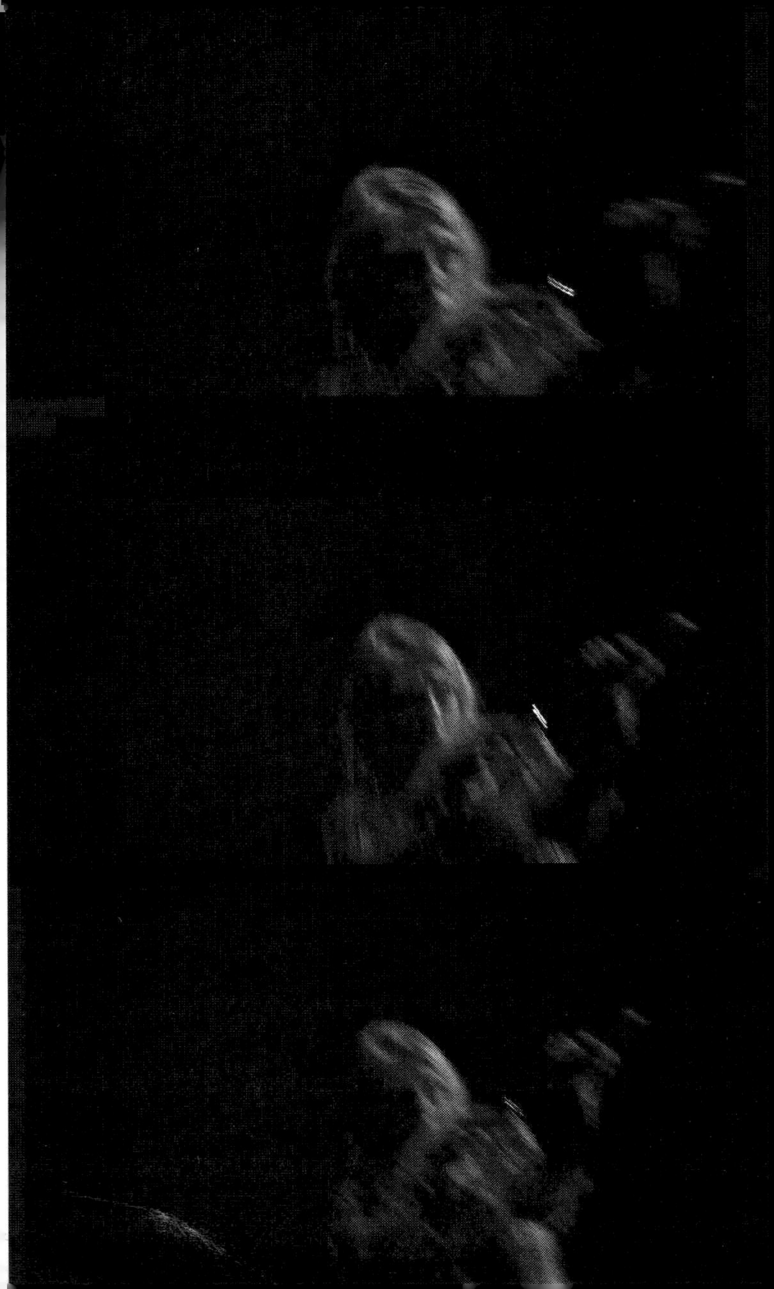

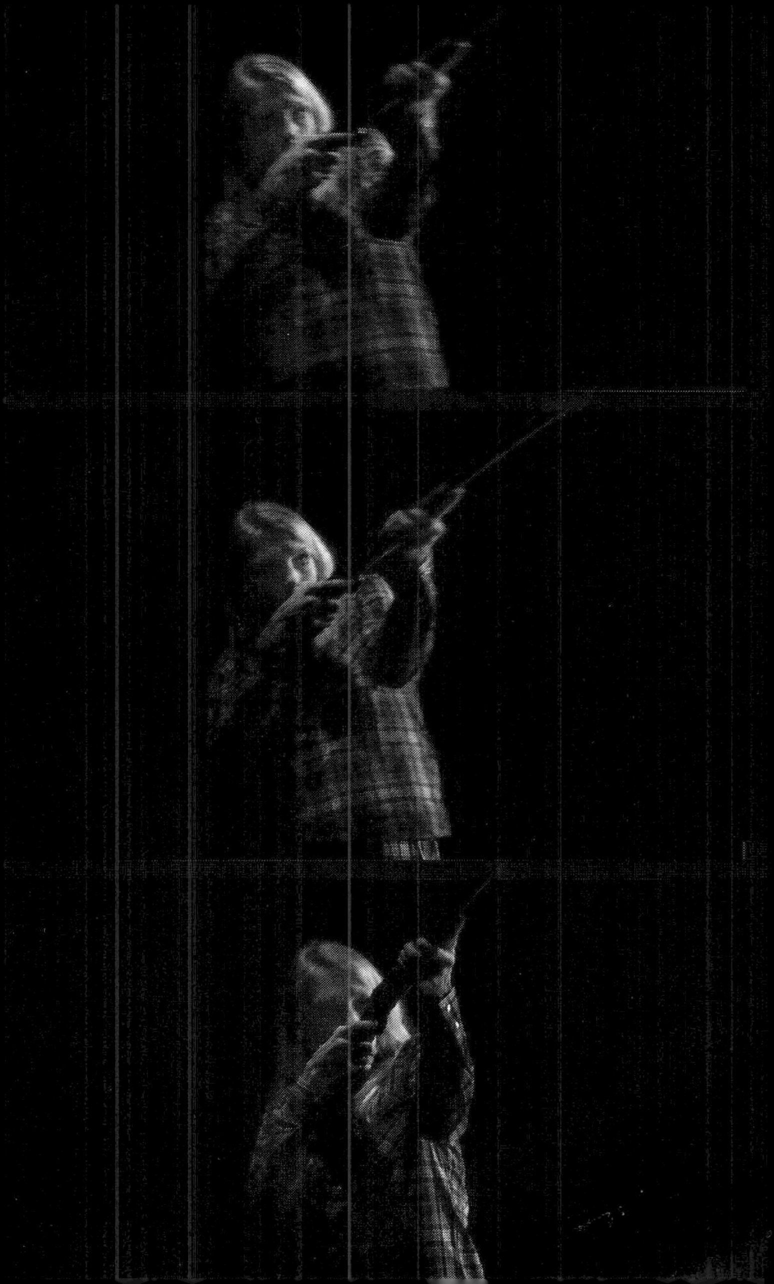

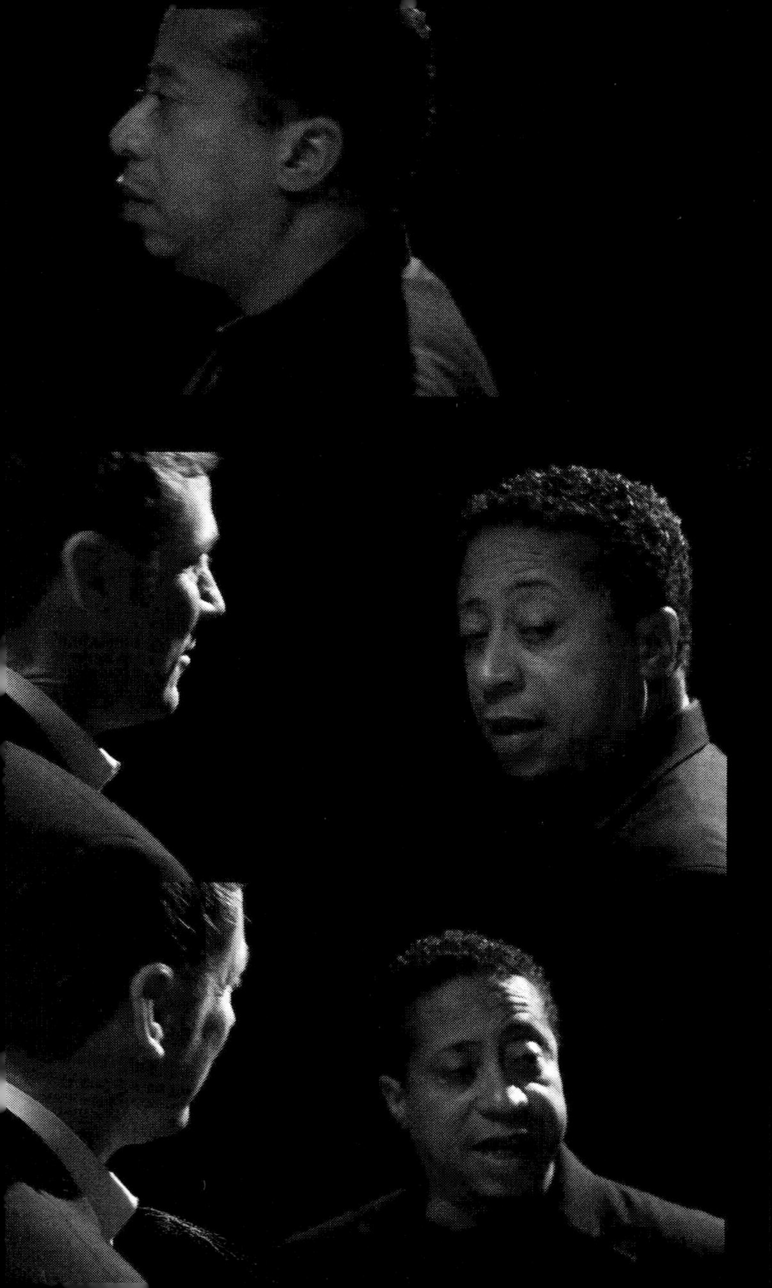

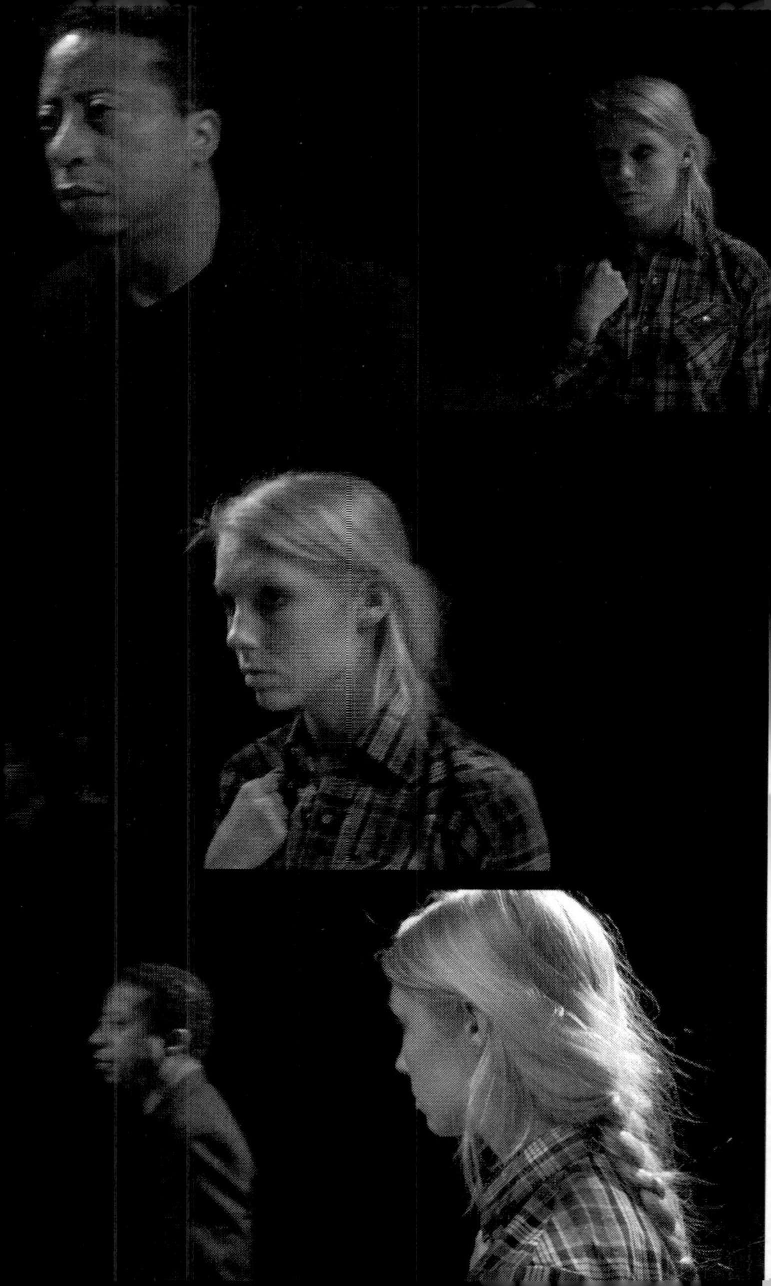

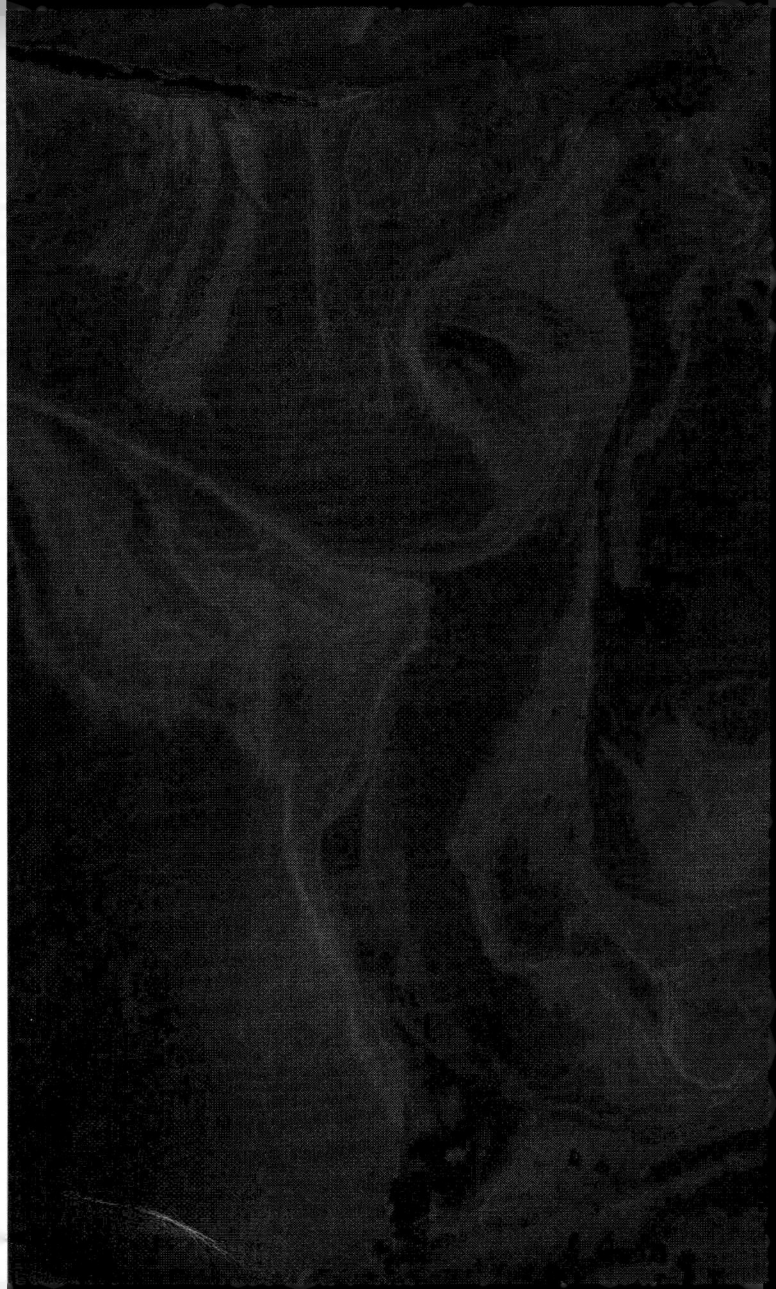

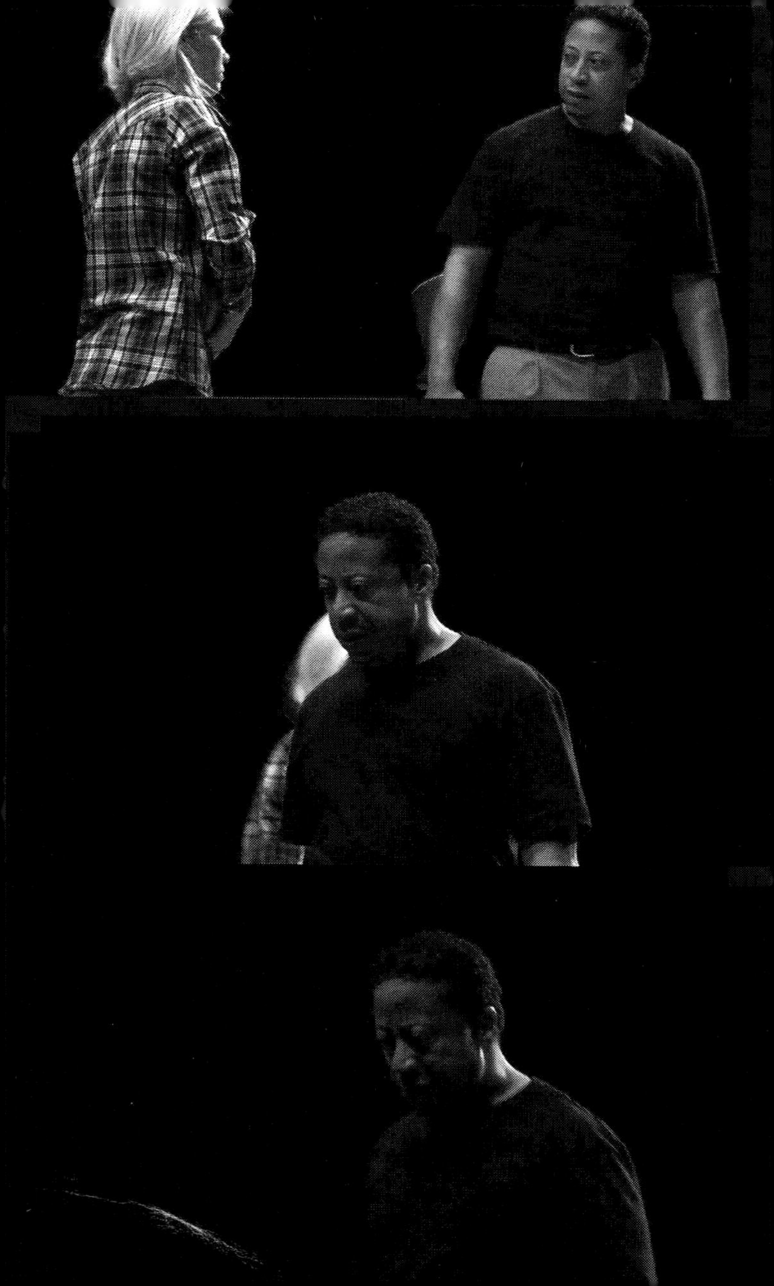

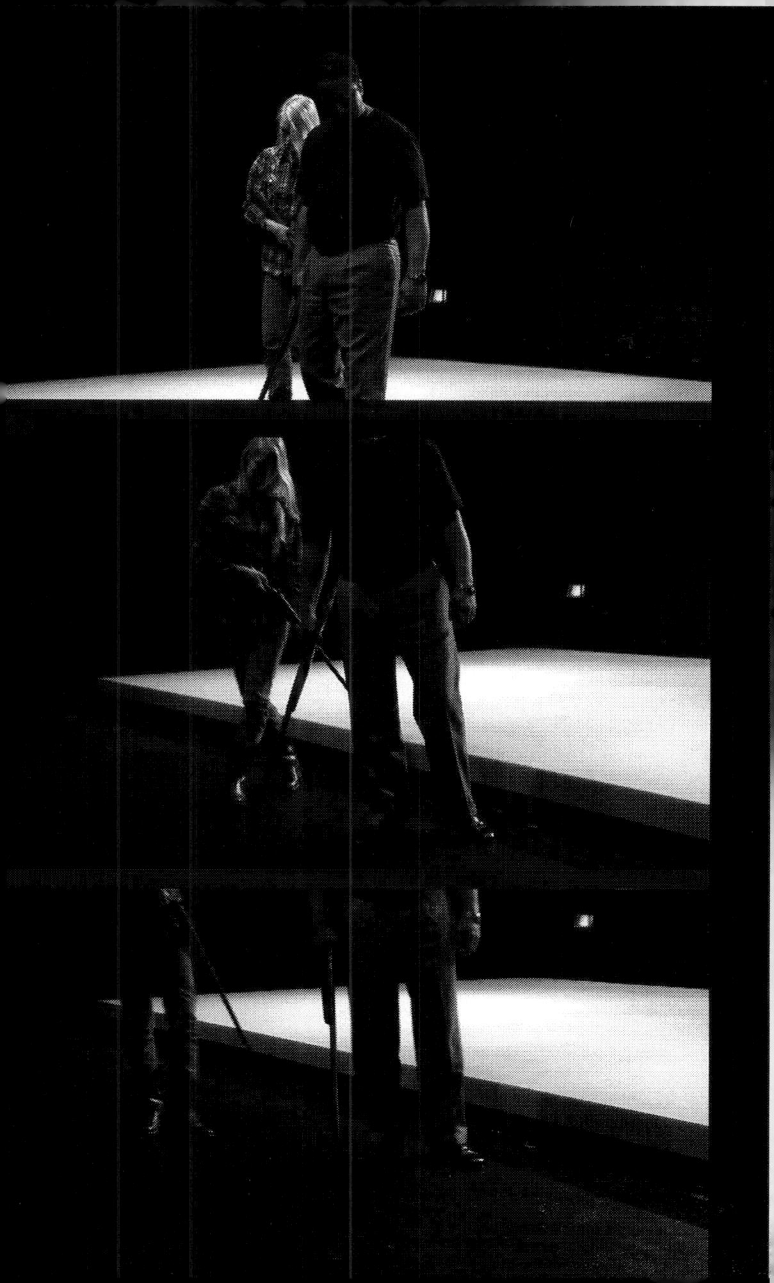

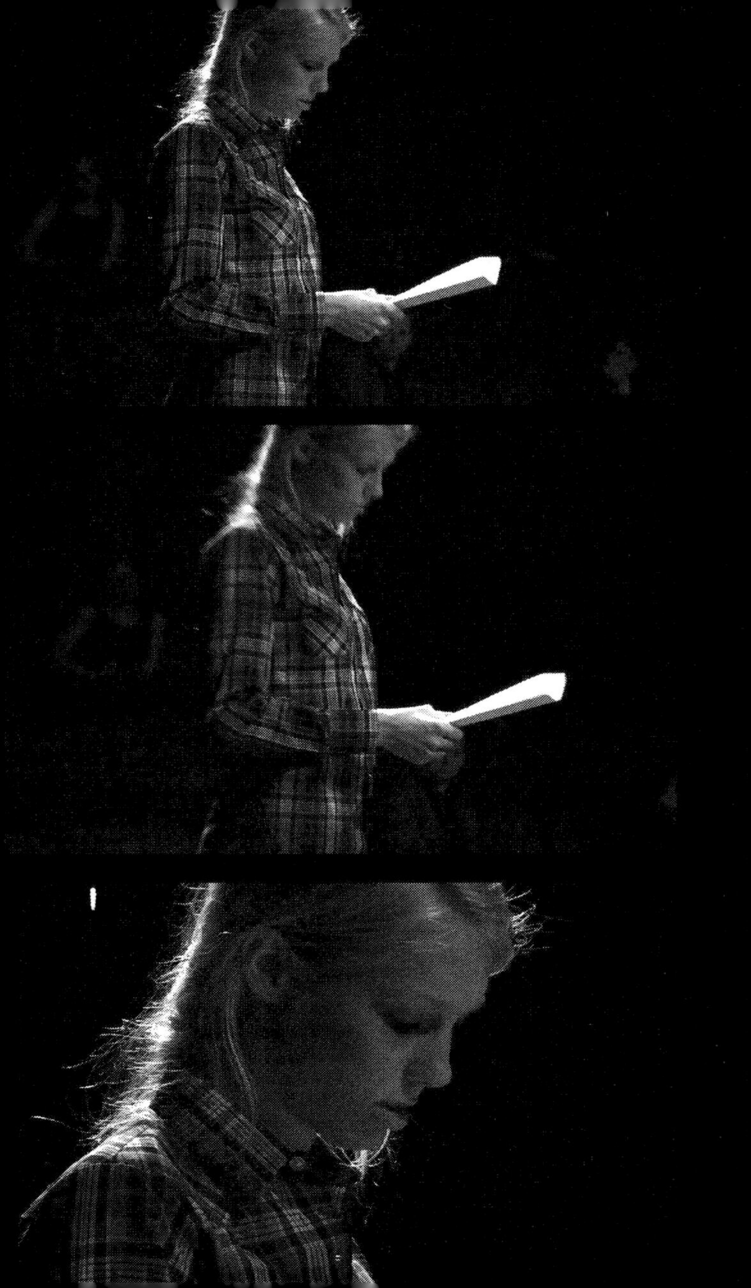

Ingo Niermann

Objects and I

The golden locks are cropped short, leaving just a hint of curl. The tight-fitting black leather jacket is at once crumpled and shiny. It can't be wet; it must be lacquered. An oil-based lacquer. Oil pumped from the gray-brown sand that stretches in dunes to the horizon— for a shiny black pipe sticks up a few yards away, bending off at right angles. Judging by its color, the sand could be mixed with oil. The sky is blue and white at the bottom, blackening steadily toward the top. It could be smoke from burning crude oil.

The blond boy's face, hair, and jacket are clean. The cropped curls and the downy beard, also blond, recall a freshly shorn lamb. He's visibly doing nothing except looking slightly sideways. Bent forward a fraction, chin raised a fraction, he appears poised to break into a run or perform a pirouette. To be stopped neither by his stiffened jacket nor by the soft ground. Even if he were waist-deep in oily mud, even if the fire had cut off all escape routes.

But first he looks, waiting for a reaction. He's not just looking to see what's going on; he's gauging the impact of his own gaze. This is mental arm-wrestling— a simple matter of more or less pressure. Goldilocks is an especially slippery opponent. His eyes are brown— almost like the sand—the pupils barely discernible. And because he never moves, he always wins no matter what. Against whom? Like the oil and the fire, the viewer is nowhere to be seen. No one stands in our way. Because the blond boy never moves, it's easy for me to practice on him, again and again.

Which makes the exercise dull: he can't see me anyway, and he wasn't looking at me even when he was still moving. I'm one of a theoretically endless number of people he didn't look at, staring instead into a camera. Perhaps he has vanished from sight amid all the smoke; perhaps he has died.

I darken my room. Were I to toss a cloth over the sun, it would be torn apart and reduced to gas, but it wouldn't catch fire. I spill refined oil. It sticks wherever there is dirt, and collects more dirt. The greater the impact of humans on the world, the more it is considered dirty, but the more it can also be cleaned. Even what the cleaning process discards as dirt can in turn be cleaned. In the ideal scenario, everything will be reused or restored, again and again. What once has lived need never die.

A photograph, on the other hand, makes something appear frozen forever. The person whose picture is taken, Roland Barthes writes, is transformed from subject to object. Along the same lines, Susan Sontag calls photography "sublimated murder."

But what is a subject anyway? What is an object? The distinction goes back to that between mind and matter. Animism is based on the assumption of two parallel spheres existing everywhere at the same time. The first is passive: what is moved can also be destroyed and is thus transient. The second is active: what does the moving is inexhaustible and thus immortal. And so the world remains in constant motion. It is guided by intent, as with conscious decision-making in humans.

Non-pantheistic religions attribute this spiritual sphere to the living alone, as an added quality.

Its purest form is found where, it is assumed, intent is particularly strong: in the human brain. This may seem paradoxical, as all earthly life—brains included—is transient. Trees live the longest, but after a thousand years at most, even they pass. It is therefore safe to assume that belief in the immortality of the spirit is there to compensate for the shock of knowing that all life will end, including our own. But physical life, too, possesses at least potential immortality, because living means renewing and reproducing oneself—though what survives is not identical, just the same or similar.

For this repetition to occur, a thing must be various in itself, since renewal that is perpetual and not simply random calls for control. Without constant reimplementation of its own programs—based, we are told, on information stored in the form of genetic code—life cannot persist.

Decoding can only take place if something has been encoded. This would require a creator, or, as Jean-Baptiste de Lamarck assumed, the genes would have to form afresh in each living thing according to its own specific features. In the case of the activation and deactivation of certain genes, this seems indeed to be the case, and only to this extent is it correct to refer to genetic information as information, but not in the case of random mutations. The fact that "genetic information" is nonetheless the standard term shows the degree to which modern science, too, is attached to the idea that all life is guided by intent, if only as an emergent quality. Meanwhile, immortality is not to be achieved until the future—with the help of science. The information process is a mediated chain reaction: the transformation of A into B initiates, by means of C,

the transformation of further As into Bs. The reproduction of life or individual cells is also a process of
information. But in this process, the so-called genetic
information is part not of the signifier but of the
signified. The processes it triggers, which cause it and
its cells to multiply, are the signifier. The information
process is not a specific phenomenon of life, but an
uncontrolled form of reproduction. The oxidation of
carbon, for example, produces heat, which causes further
carbon to oxidize. This fast-spreading oxidation information is known as fire. Rising smoke, on the other hand,
tells me there is a fire — insofar as the correspondence
between actual fire and my mental image of fire is
assumed to be adequate. But such an assumption can
only be made by someone capable of becoming me,
or of interpreting my thought on the basis of the
underlying physical information processes. Where our
notion of information has its origins — in conscious
communication with oneself and others—is precisely
where it is hardest to verify.

With assumptions like atomic orbitals and the
uncertainty principle, physics has long since called
into question whether solid objects exist at all outside
our minds. The fact that information processing
operates with a simplified assumption of solidity can
be explained in functional terms. But how can one
experience consistent form consciously? The obvious
answer is: consciousness only exists at all to the extent
that similarity pertains. And since consciousness can
also observe and influence itself, it is not epiphenomenal;
it is an elementary force.

Science faces the problem that it has long been able
to explain intelligent life without the phenomenon of

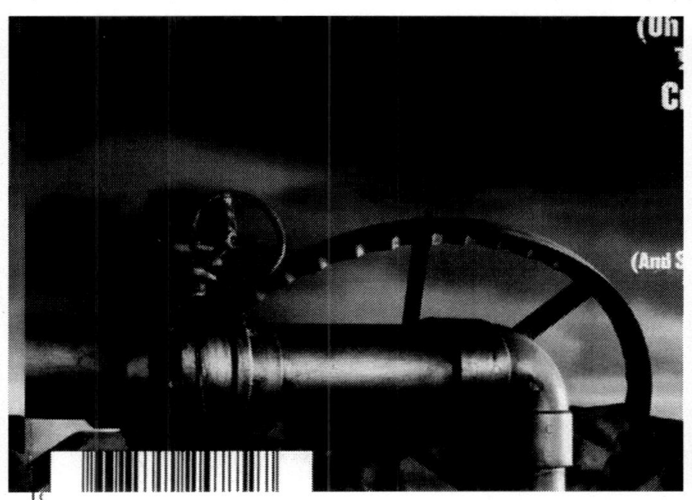

consciousness. Sure enough, consciousness exists, so it is credited with the role of assuring a lasting identity: while the brain gets on with its work, the mind tries hard to create a retrospective semblance of continuous deliberation. But for whom? For the mind alone? The snake eats its own tail. In any case, or so it seems, the ability to create artificial consciousness will not make or break the creation of artificial intelligence.

With the link between life and information already severed, it makes sense to also sever that between consciousness and higher intelligence, and to under-stand consciousness not as an emergent phenomenon but as an elementary one. This does not mean a return to animism, which attributed consciousness to objects, but, following an anthropocentric view, associating consciousness exclusively with intelligence and life. Panpsychism, the usual term for the view of consciousness as an elementary phenomenon, is misleading as it is

traditionally used as an umbrella term grouping
animist-related, pantheist, and hylozoist positions.
To distance themselves from this, some philosophers
of mind also speak of panexperientialism, panprotoex-
perientialism, or panprotopsychism.

Beyond the problem of reconciling general relativity
and quantum mechanics, then, both must now also
be reconciled with the existence of consciousness. One
approach, as advocated by Roger Penrose, is to understand consciousness as an intrinsic quality of mysterious
physical phenomena such as quantum entanglement.
This view is attractive, as it is used for advanced information processing in the form of quantum computers
and quantum cryptography, implying an elementary
connection between consciousness and information
processing. But although it contradicts classical laws
of causality, this information processing occurs only in
isolated instances.

Considering the obstinacy with which consciousness
resists any interpretation in terms of physics, as well
as the apparent unreliability of the laws of physics
themselves, I must ask myself why I don't begin by
assuming only my own consciousness as given. There
may be others alongside mine. And there may even be
a physical world, but one that depends on consciousness.
Not consciousness but the physical world is the emergent
phenomenon, then, becoming increasingly concrete the
more it is perceived. Being is being perceived.

It is thus possible that I, too, exist only as long as I
am perceived by others. Even, if need be, by objects.
Which I in turn look at to ensure they do not disappear.
Coexistence is not an exalted ideal, but an inevitable
routine. Fortunately, the world is so full that I need not

worry about suddenly vanishing. Especially since inert matter cannot decide whether or not to pay attention. It does so incessantly — like the blond boy — which makes it appear undemanding and thus inferior. Objects are dependable. Whereas humans and animals can shut their eyes, turn their heads, bury themselves, or run away, objects simply need to be put with other objects and handled with care. And when I no longer exist, my body can be preserved in such a way that it survives as an object.

In her film *About the object* (2009), inspired by a journey to Cairo and the Egyptian pyramids, Amy Patton asks two actresses to behave like an object talking to itself in a vitrine.

A: Maybe just like... um... for this character you're basically an object in a vitrine. In a museum. For some reason I always imagine it a bit more...it's almost like you're speaking but no one can hear you. Almost like an interior monologue.
B: Okay. Do you want me to not move as much? Or...
I guess I'm not really moving that much anyway.
A: I think that's fine because you're in a vitrine. I mean, it's hard because you're an object, I mean you're an object and not a character. It's hard to know the object's motivations.
B: Right. So less, like, telling someone else and more just to myself?
A: Yeah! You're totally just like... you're an object ruminating in a vitrine. In the Met.
B: Okay. Well that makes sense.
A: Well, yeah, more or less.

How is a human being supposed to actually be an object, rather than merely posing, object-like, for a photograph that captures the moment? A film, too, is a sequence of individual photographs, but so rapid that humans are unable to consciously perceive them as separate. Even if it were possible to pose individually for each frame, there would still be the transitions. A sentence is a sequence of words that take time to be spoken; but to think and understand each of them takes a single moment. They don't even need to be written down to be turned into objects. And even objects that are not words themselves are capable of evoking words. A flower, whether alive or made of plastic (and thus from oil), not only says its name, but also tells me: "Yellow." To a bee, it calls out: "Great sex, right here!" In the same way, the whole sentence is also an object. The whole paragraph. The whole page.

I walk around and new sentences constantly come into being around me. Even without seeing, hearing, or smelling them I can read them and write them. Just as life can be created out of genes, so, too, thoughts can be materialized automatically. All I need to know is how to activate the mechanism. In the case of physical reproduction, this means sex. Procreation by thought alone has been given a name, too: it's called magic. One shouldn't be discouraged if it doesn't work straight away. Sex doesn't lead to conception every time either. And there is such a thing as a mental miscarriage.

One basic mistake is to begin by speaking words that are then supposed to bring about the desired effect, instead of speaking the desired effect into being directly. That's what magic's all about.

Perhaps it's the same kind of shame we experience with regard to sex that keeps us from practicing magic. Of course, it's also extremely dangerous. If knowledge of sexual reproduction weren't already so widespread, wouldn't you hesitate to even mention it?

But here I'm alone. What there is here I cannot see. I close my eyes, and the blackness becomes fuzzy. Not even the blackness is really there any more. I stick my fingers into my ears and hear a quiet whistling, from no particular direction, but it can only be coming from my head. A basic operating tone: machines drone, heads whistle. I smell the oil that forms a thin layer on the objects. Murkily golden, with a greenish hue, iridescent. Like the devil's piss. I don't need to see it. I can't see air either.

Many religions assume air to be spiritual—it is transparent, has no odor, and doesn't fall, but must be constantly breathed in and out in order for us to remain alive. Today we know that combustion requires both oxygen and carbon. Carbon for which we kill other life or which we brutally tear from the earth. Only the energy released by combustion is weightless, and it can drive everything: muscles, brains, and machines. Ultimately including machines that are driven by nature-given energy and that shape nature just as we want it. And when some want it one way and others another, then the two groups simply keep the necessary distance.

Until this comes to pass, I remain in the dark, at most looking at this photograph of the curly-haired blond stuck in a lifeless landscape, his expression so gentle, as if constantly aware that he, too, must soon die. And a great peace comes over me.

Translated from the German by Nicholas Grindell

...just right, for Dad had copies of the "logs" of every one of...

young man exactly what he had done over at Lobos River with...

Stubbs Fishkill number so on.

Then the postman would come, bringing reports from all the...

...tryin' to do anything for people that ain't got sense enough...

take care of their own fingers, to say nothing of their heads? B...

...scratches on their faces!" So Dad would... his favorite...

theme, the shiftlessness of the working class whom he had to em...

...struck. First, they had lost a set of tools, and then, while they wer...

and "fishing" is merely...that...taught. C...d "like the...

...jinx in that hole, they had "jammed" three times, and they wer...

the well every couple of hours all day, but nothing doing; they trie...

...but in vain. The hole would... in on them, and they had to clea...

and fish ahead, over afresh. They had caught the tools and jarre...

them out, but the crowbar was still down there, wedged fast...

The third evening, Dad said he guessed they'd... even over...

Lobos River; it was time to get a new casing anyhow, and he like...

...fellows. Bunny jumped up, saying, "T...k...

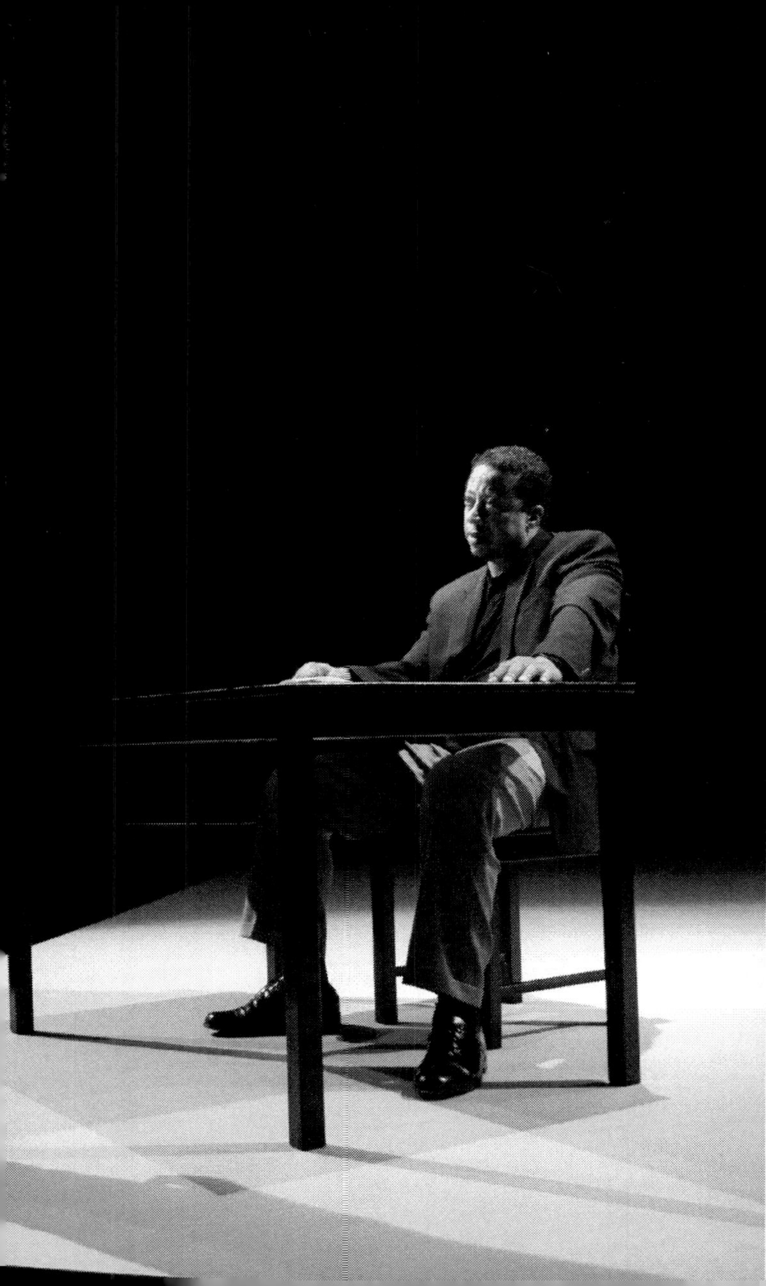

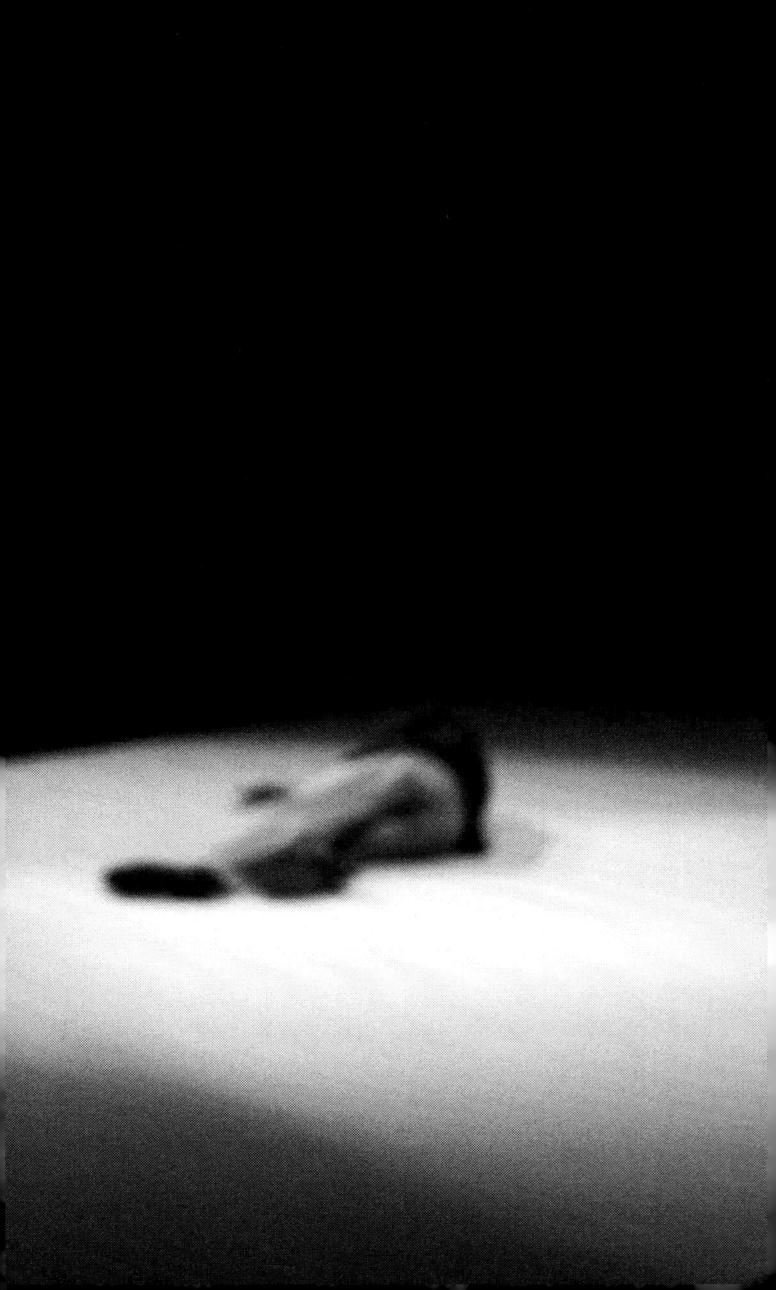

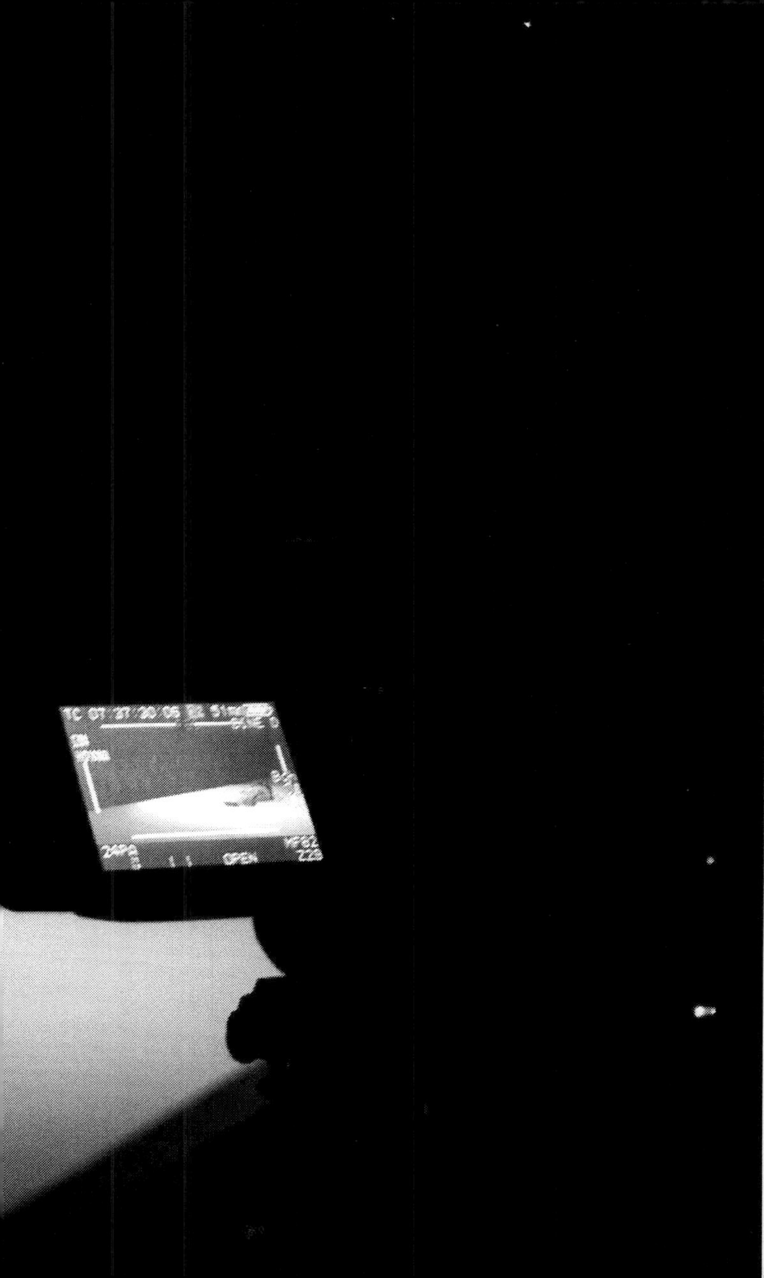

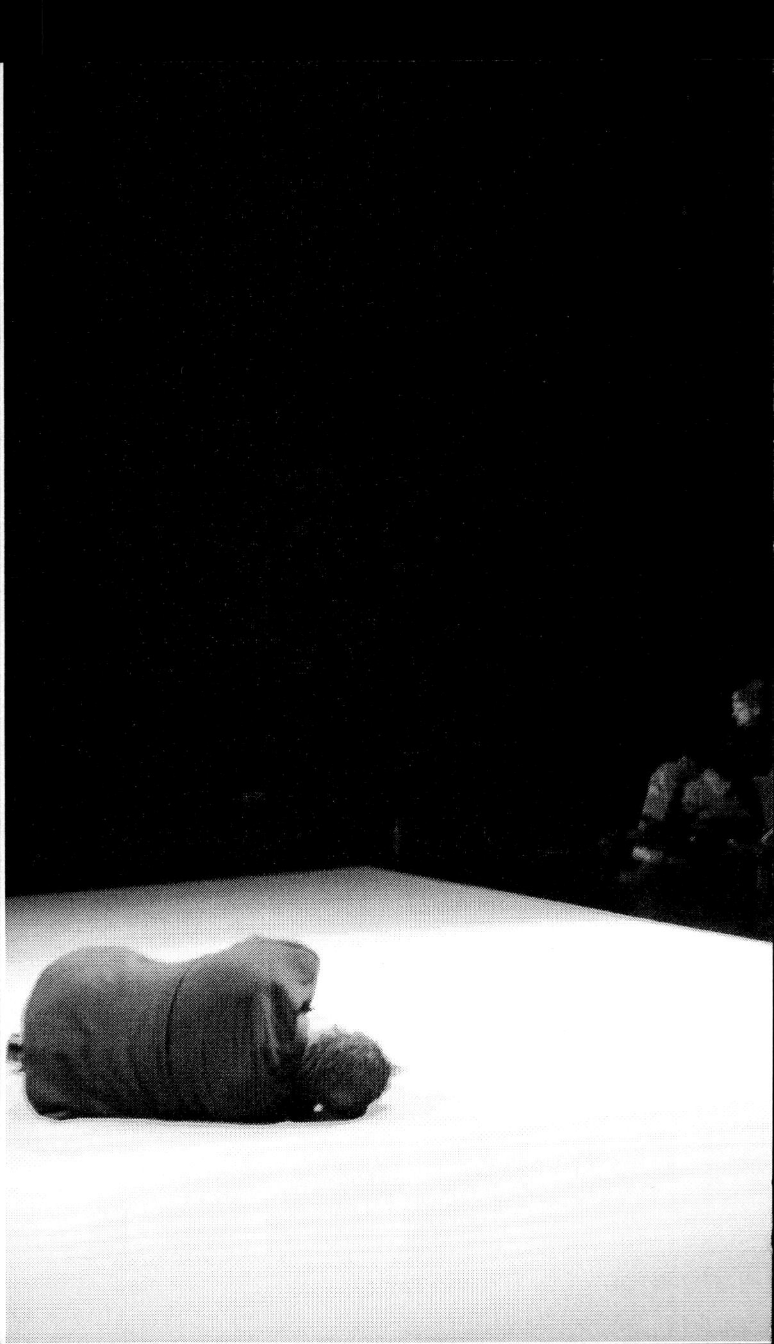

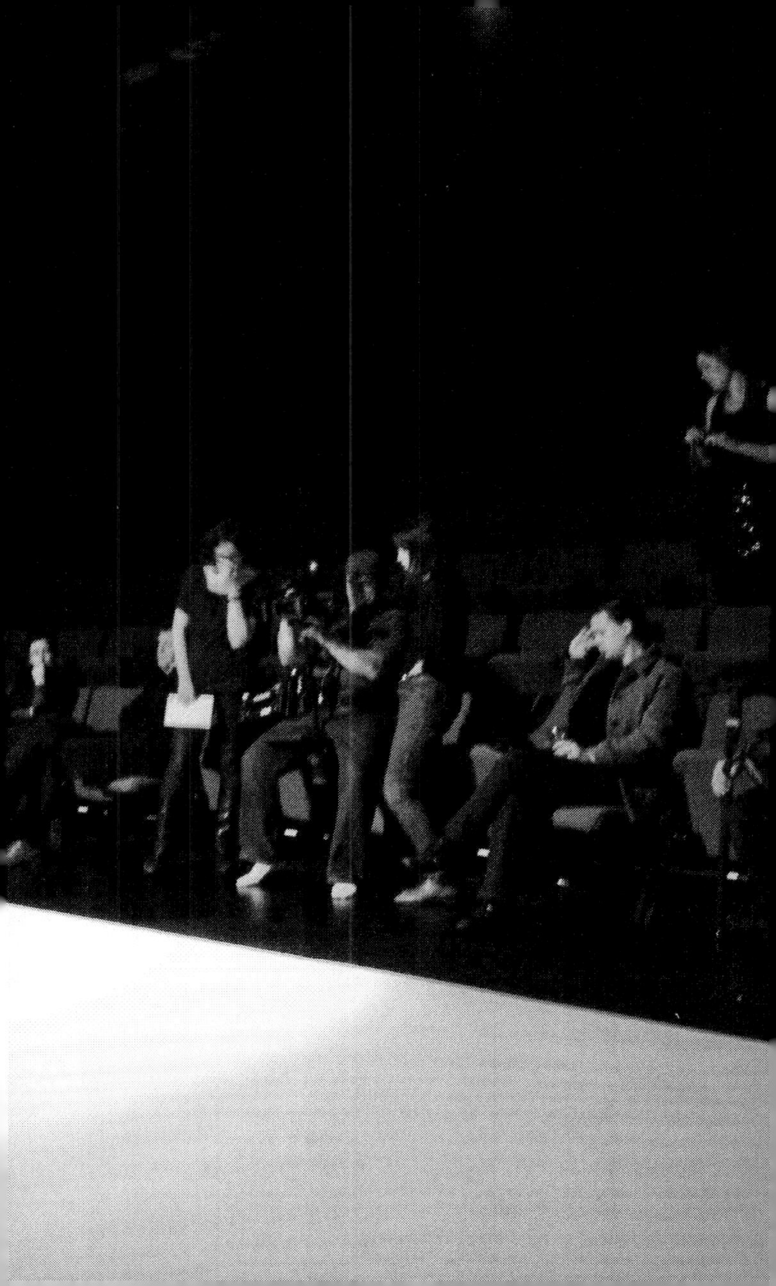

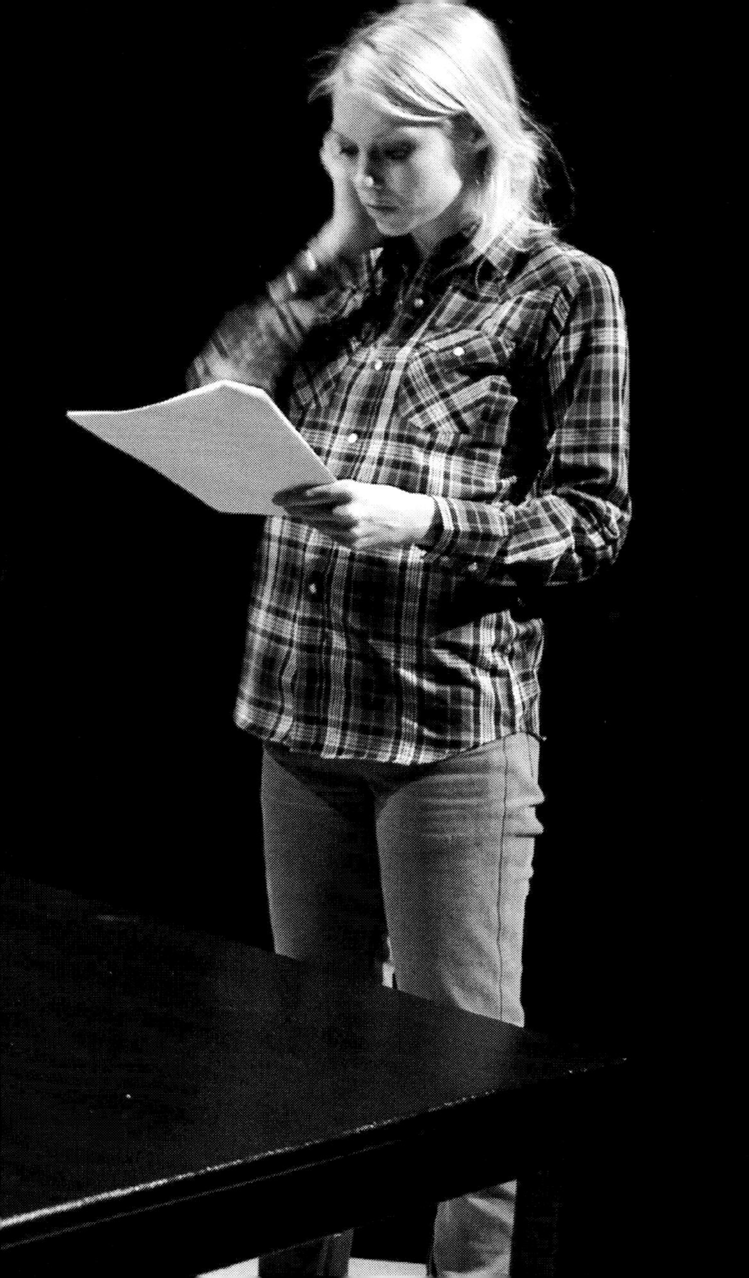

Rachel Hooper

Stories Told in the Shape of a Sphere

Amy Patton's films have a way of sticking with you. Years after first seeing them, I find myself still thinking back and trying to put together all the pieces of their dream-like fictions woven within tightly edited structures. One that I often return to is *A Satisfied Mind* (2005), which I first encountered at the space the Brooklyn gallery Pierogi operated at the time in Leipzig, Germany. In the film, the narrator is an anesthetized psychosurgery patient named Jeff Morrow. As Morrow is operated on, he remembers a Greyhound bus inspector whose relentlessly hyperactive memory drives him to commit suicide one day by blowing up the bus on which he is riding. The only person who can lead us to where it happened, we're told, is a woman with a severe case of amnesia. Inexplicably, the exploding bus is replaced by a crashing plane, exposing "a secret form of time."

Divided into two parts on a split screen, *A Satisfied Mind* is spliced together from pieces of 16mm footage that the Berlin-based, Texan-born Patton found tangled up in a garbage bag in Austin. The filmmaker essentially "hijacked," to use her term, the source material of amnesia studies, children traveling on a Greyhound bus, and aviation disasters to create her own story, using voiceover to pull together these fragments. The richly textured and color-saturated stock is scratched and sometimes jumpy; in contrast, Patton's slow

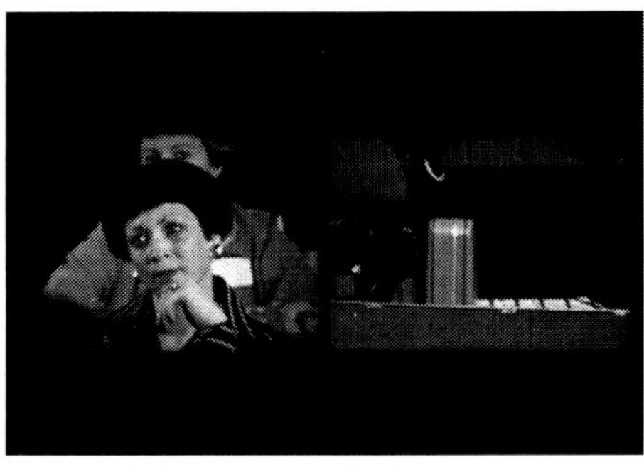

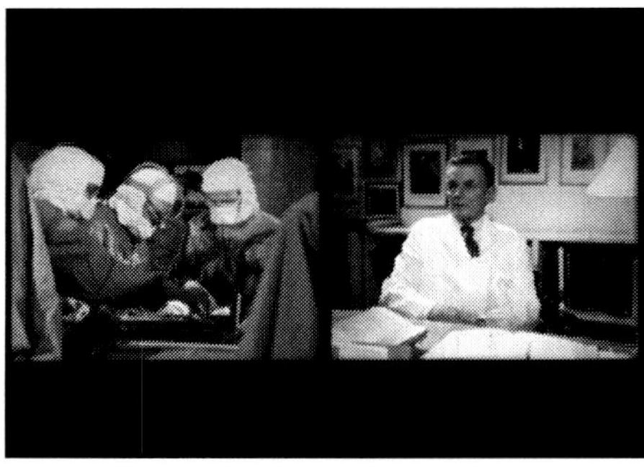

Stills from *A Satisfied Mind*, 2005.
Video (color, sound), 4:32 min.

and even editing creates a pace that allows for subtle connections between what is happening simultaneously on the two sides of the screen. The relationship between appropriated films and the artist's text raises an unnamed question or expectation that seems to drive the plot forward, even as the testimony of a woman without memory and the disturbance of plane crashes deny any logical progression.[1]

1. The questions that the viewer is prompted to ask may drive the suspense of the films as well. See Noël Carroll, *Theorizing the Moving Image* (New York: Cambridge University Press, 1996), 94–113.

When I came to work at Blaffer Art Museum, a year after I saw *A Satisfied Mind* in Leipzig, I wondered how the film might be received in Texas, where it originated. As it turns out, when I moved to Houston, Patton had just written and directed another 16mm film with Texan connections, *Chronicle of a Demise* (2006). The measured, quiet atmosphere of this film brings out the formal composition of each shot, the dynamic beauty of trains in motion, roads receding in the distance, and rolling waves. The narrator explains that the film is a report by "the Center" on surveillance of "the poet," who lives in his uncle's basement outside Dallas, and that the Center is "reluctant to release the following images" given the charges against it. The charges are never fully explained. The narrator goes on to say that evidence has been tampered with, footage of the Berlin Zoo and a European port are mixed in with shots of homogeneous aluminum-sided homes taken in Hutto, Texas. At the end, the narrator explains that the Center will be dissolved and "no individual members of this organization will be at liberty to discuss the poet's actions or whereabouts."

The narrator's speech in both *A Satisfied Mind* and *Chronicle of a Demise* binds the flow of images in each film into one story with beginning, middle, and end, as it would in a literary work. Patton's characters are themselves derivations from published short stories and novels: the man plagued by a photographic memory in *A Satisfied Mind* is based on Ireneo Funes from the Jorge Luis Borges short story "Funes, the Memorious" (1942) and the narrator of *Chronicle of a Demise* on the protagonist of a Tennessee Williams short story of the same name (1967). As with their

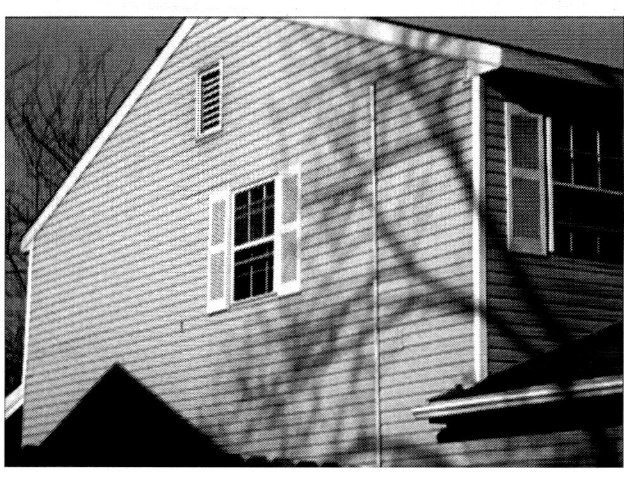

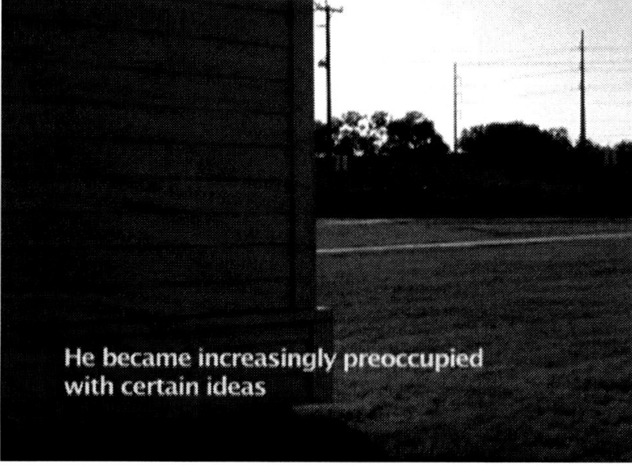

together, and the middle-sized girl, who went by the name of Mee-

42

lie
an
an

wa
an
a p

]
sai
rel
"le
figi
bro
'
'
'
'
]
sai
'
not
"
"W
pre
put
"
der
frie
the
"
awa
ool
her
ie {
S
ier

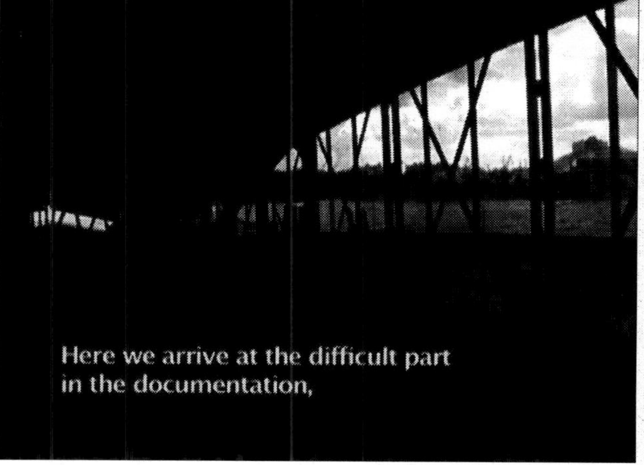

Stills from *Chronicle of a Demise*, 2006. 16mm film transferred to video (color, sound), 8:23 min.

literary counterparts, we trust the narrators in Patton's films to provide authoritative accounts of what they observe. Patton uses the narrators to represent what Michel Chion calls the "I-voice," the speaker inside our heads who tells us our own thoughts. As Chion explains, the "I-voice" is an off-screen performer speaking so closely into the mike that there are no reverberations and the voice resonates in us "as if it were our own voice, like a voice in the first person."[2] In Patton's two films, the narrating voice, along with the often static point of view of the camera, suggests this first-person structure.

Patton's work is also informed by the legacy of structural film, as well as structural and post-structural theory in general. Two of her earliest films—*I Have Two Dreams* (2000) and *Dream of a Contraption* (2000)—show her interest in the psychological intensity of structural filmmaking techniques such as mathematically determined edits and extended mise-en-scènes. At the University of Texas in Austin, where Patton made these films and earned a degree in art history, the Polish filmmaker Bogdan Perzynski introduced her to surrealist films, Sergei Eisenstein's montage technique, Michael Snow's experimental films, and videos of Bruce Nauman's early perform-ances. Once she moved to Germany she continued studying experimental film and media design at the Universität der Künste Berlin with Stan Douglas, Heinz Emigholz, and Maria Vedder. Her films continue to reflect the tradition of what P. Adams Sitney has

2. Michel Chion, *The Voice in Cinema*, trans. Claudia Gorbman (New York: Columbia University Press, 1999), 51.

described as "a cinema of structure in which the shape of the whole film is predetermined and simplified, [which gives] the primal impression of the film."[3]

Patton's films thus have a distinct, predetermined shape established by the voiceover and the use of found and documentary footage. Their set shape is reinforced by her tight editing and slow, steady shots. However, this ostensibly straightforward structure is interrupted and subverted by narrative overlaps, slippages, and echoes. Three-quarters of the way through *A Satisfied Mind*, the narration changes from a first-person recollection to a direct address of the viewer, who is told that the woman with amnesia is "the one who can lead you to the spot where it happened." At the very end of the film, the narrator describes the events as belonging to the distant past: "Historians maintain that the pilot and the dreamer had nothing to do with each other, but I imagine they're just trying to cover the fact that these parallelisms between a certain pilot's fate in 1929 and the fate of that bus in 1968 could suppose a secret form of time: a pattern of repeating lines." These shifts subtly undermine the coherence and authority of the narrator, as does the sometimes disjunctive relationship between what he says and the images we see, as when a plane takes off inexplicably on the right side of the screen as the woman without a memory leaves a secretarial school on the left. Likewise, *Chronicle of a Demise* begins with the narrator describing the images we are watching and how they relate to the subject of his investigation, the poet. But once we are

3. P. Adams Sitney, *Visionary Film: The American Avant-Garde, 1943–2000* (Cary, NC: Oxford University Press, 2002), 348.

11,17,18,23,24,26,27,28,35, 38,39 40,48,49
50,51, 62

11,17,18,23,24,26,27,28,35, 38,39 40,48,49
50,51, 62

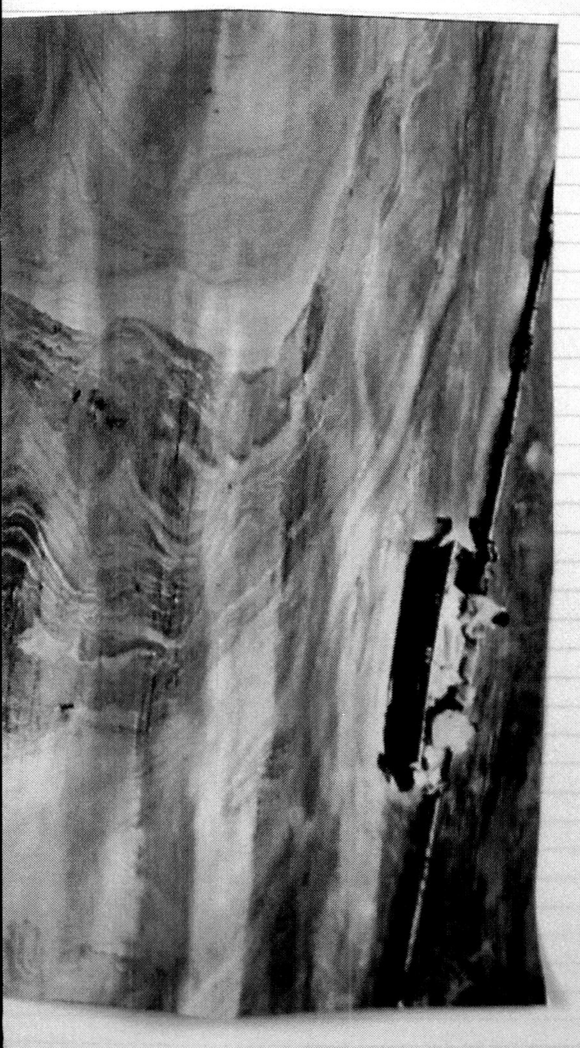

(nothing happens exactly, not
in the "traditional" sense)

little

COLOR

I need [...]
[...] I could do everything
easily
repeats the same thing she
says in the voiceover
blunt → acting / real / script
→ non-script
→ audience feedback to
producer
→ out of focus OK
disappearing act
audience filling their seats
me. I used to
be me. I'm not me

photographs / more
voice over "they want
to be loved, they have to be
photograph[ed]
audience

the wildcat
~~the Exposure~~ Audience?
The Exposure
the rebel / interviews?
the Revelation
Audience
The Ride
The Penalty
The Strike

Imagined

Bunny voice-over

wildcat

CASSAVETES   SINCLAIR
- play 5 act structure
- revolution
- lines in head, in
  context, out loud

audience looking
photography

black film

6/9/10

① WILDCAT   5 RANCH
② EXPOSURE
  — photograph
③ Rebel
  — interviews   4 Penalty
④ Revelation
⑥
⑦ Strike

Audience.

psychedelic?
Rebel.

christoph → wed or thurs   13-14 hr.

→ missing shots of the <u>audience</u>
   (could be a sinema <u>audience</u>)

→ audience appears and disappears

→ it's about buny/mia subjectivity,
   slippage of the mind

→ as if she's remembering it, piecing
   the experience together in her
   head. sometimes it's just in her
   head

→ quick cuts away → like ~~thoughts~~
   hide camera fuckups

→ from the perspective of ???

→ repeats things she says in v.o.

gun shot
car door
trunk close

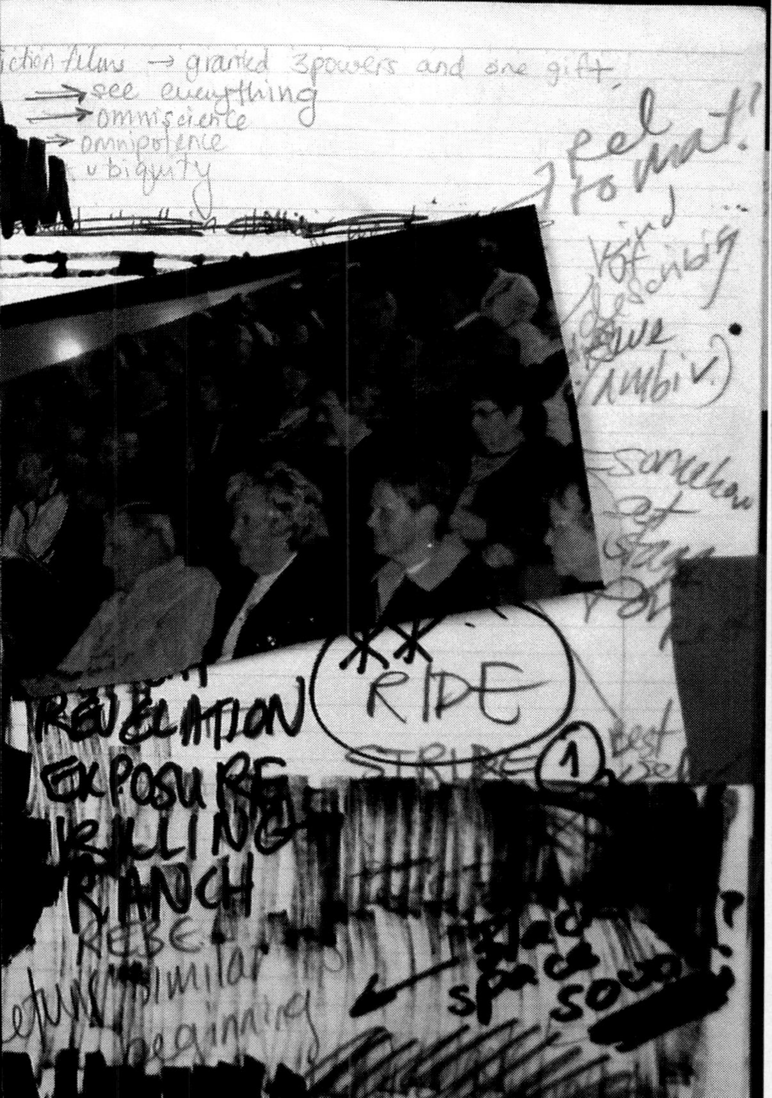

ction film → granted 3 powers and one gift
→ see everything
→ omniscience
→ omnipotence
→ ubiquity

REVELATION
EXPOSURE
KILLING
RANCH
REBE...

RIDE
STRIP (1)

into the film, the narrator explains that his documentation has been tampered with, and that "it is not our
material, but that of an impostor."

Breaks in the direction established by Patton's
narrators create a tension as the stories progress.[4]
We are compelled to watch the films again and again
in an attempt to resolve their incongruities. Raymond
Bellour has written about the "repetition-resolution
effect" of Hollywood cinema, in which rhyming and
parallels in a film are used to resolve the narrative.
For example, many Hollywood films end in the same
place where they started. As Bellour explains, such
conventions carry "narrative difference through the
ordered network of resemblances; by unfolding
symmetries (with varying degrees of refinement) they
bring out the dissymmetry without which there would
be no narrative. . . . [The film] is constantly repeating
itself because it is resolving itself."[5] Although Patton's
films also incorporate repetitions and parallels, her
work does not offer a tidy sense of resolution. Instead,
we are left searching, watching the looped films, and
waiting for the repetitions to deliver an answer.

As *A Satisfied Mind* moves from memory to dream
logic, and as the authority of the narrator is gradually
dismantled in *Chronicle of a Demise*, we wonder whether
the films are documentary or fantasy, fact or fiction,
dream or reality. Patton has said that she wants to
create confusion to prevent the viewer's suspension of
disbelief: "I want the viewer to remember that I might

4. Barthes would say that the suspense in the film relates directly to its
structure: "Suspense, therefore, is a game with structure, designed to
endanger and glorify it." Roland Barthes, *Image-Music-Text* (New York:
Hill and Wang, 1977), 119.

also be an unreliable narrator, and everything framing the work might also be untrustworthy."[6] Ultimately, we are left to determine for ourselves what truth there is behind the films.

I first met Amy Patton when she stopped in Houston in 2008 on her way home to Austin for a visit. At the time, she was working on *About the object*—a project involving voice and a videotaped performance—for CCS Bard with Christina Linden (who two years earlier was working at Pierogi where she introduced me to Patton's work). Patton explained that she had started working with actors, using voice recordings, improvisations, and reenactments to engage the artificiality of theater and film. As the Cynthia Woods Mitchell Center Fellow, I invited her to work with actors from the University of Houston through the Mitchell Center, where she was in residency for the month of January 2010 the UH School of Theatre & Dance not only collaborated with her creatively, but also served as an invaluable partner and resource for production of the resulting film, *Oil*. Patton shot the film in a black box theater in the School of Theatre & Dance, where she built a simple set—a raised platform, a black table, and a few black chairs—and worked with a cast of six actors to develop characters and choreograph scenes built on brief quotations from Upton Sinclair's novel *Oil!* (1927). *Oil* plays with the discordance between Sinclair's material and the

5. Raymond Bellour, "Segmenting/Analyzing," in Philip Rosen, ed., *Narrative, Apparatus, Ideology: A Film Theory Reader* (New York: Columbia University Press, 1986), 66.

6. Amy Patton, e-mail message to the author, April 4, 2010.

experiences of the actors and artist in making the film. It is part filmed theatre piece and part documentation of the making of the film, a sort-of pseudo-rehearsal shot with a single Steadicam. Memory and self-determined identity and perception are important themes in this new work, as they were in *A Satisfied Mind* and *Chronicle of a Demise*. Patton's excerpts from Sinclair's

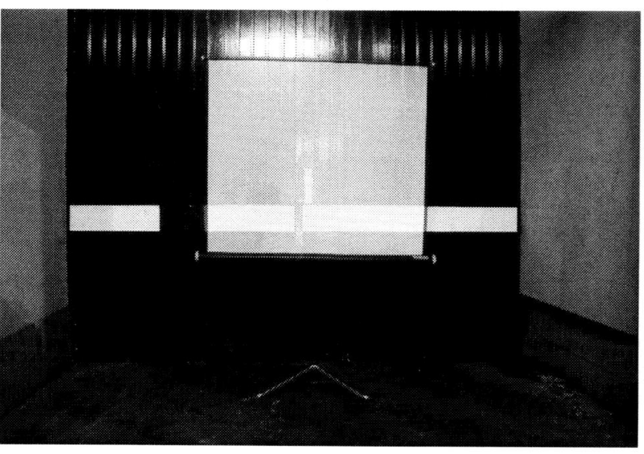

Untitled (Bergmannstrasse), 2005. Projected photograph on screen, C-print, 17 3/4 x 23 5/8 in. (45 x 60 cm)

book describe the involvement of "Dad" and "Bunny" in the oil industry, their relationship with the neighboring Watkins family, and Bunny's rejection of the oil industry and embrace of the Socialist movement. Patton was struck by how far removed we are from the history being described in Sinclair's novel, particularly its socialist agenda, yet how intimately related our current values and political realities are to those at the onset of the Great Depression. The film, exploring the reinterpretation of historical material as it has been organized to fit our present self-identity, manifests her interest in appropriation as a function of memory. In *Oil*, she not only repurposes a historical text, Sinclair's *Oil!*, but refers to another contemporary production derived from it—Paul Thomas Anderson's *There Will Be Blood* (2007)—which the actors subtly reference in their performances.

Patton's solo exhibition at Blaffer brings together her three films—*A Satisfied Mind*, *Chronicle of a Demise*, and *Oil*. Layering images and narratives that continually double-back and intersect, these works together ask: Is there such a thing as objective observation, or is the construction of fictitious identities an essential part of perception? We are tantalized by the illusion of objectivity, but Patton reminds us repeatedly of its impossibility. As we write our own stories about what we see, what are we inventing and what are we omitting? Do our explanations and rationalizations conceal as much as they reveal?

Patton had addressed these questions in a series of photographic "studies" she made in 2005 at the same time she was working on *A Satisfied Mind*. The images in the photographs are banal—the tile wall at an airport, translucent curtains on a floor-to-ceiling window looking out onto the street, the striped wall of a subway station. Though the locations are places where people meet, conversations take place, and episodes of all sorts occur, the photographs record moments when nothing was happening. After some event did take place, Patton installed a portable screen at the site and projected onto it the image of her original photograph. She then photographed the projection, thus presenting "before" and "after" without giving any evidence of the intervening

occurrence. A new series of photographs that Patton is
creating for the exhibition at Blaffer—showing a bright
spectrum of colors refracted on the surfaces of pools of
oil—abstracts this idea even further. The oil, created
through a process of refinement, could be interpreted as
a metaphor for memory, a repository of ephemeral
images that constantly reinvents and redefines itself.

Consulting my own memories to write this account
of Amy Patton's work, I sense my overlapping experiences
of time. As when watching Patton's films, I feel that I
am going in circuitous paths and am left wondering if
what I've omitted in my story might be just as important
as what I've recorded. Life is fraught with coincidences,
and in many ways this book and exhibition at Blaffer
and Patton's residency at the Mitchell Center have been
an amalgamation of accidental, or perhaps intuitively
motivated, intersections. What you read here and what
you see in the galleries is a result not only of Amy
Patton's hard work and distinctive vision, but also of her
collaboration with Blaffer and Mitchell Center staff,
contributors to the book, and makers of *Oil*.

We each offered our subjective takes on what we
were experiencing and making, and we constructed and
unraveled connections between us as we worked together
to achieve our common goals. To me, this is the secret
form of time that Patton's films disclose, one in which
experience is created as much as it is passively taken in.

The title of this essay was inspired by Sergei Eisenstein's statement that
"I dream of creating a book in the shape of a sphere," quoted by Anne
Nesbet in her *Savage Junctures: Sergei Eisenstein and the Shape of Thinking*
(London and New York: I. B. Tauris, 2007), 206.

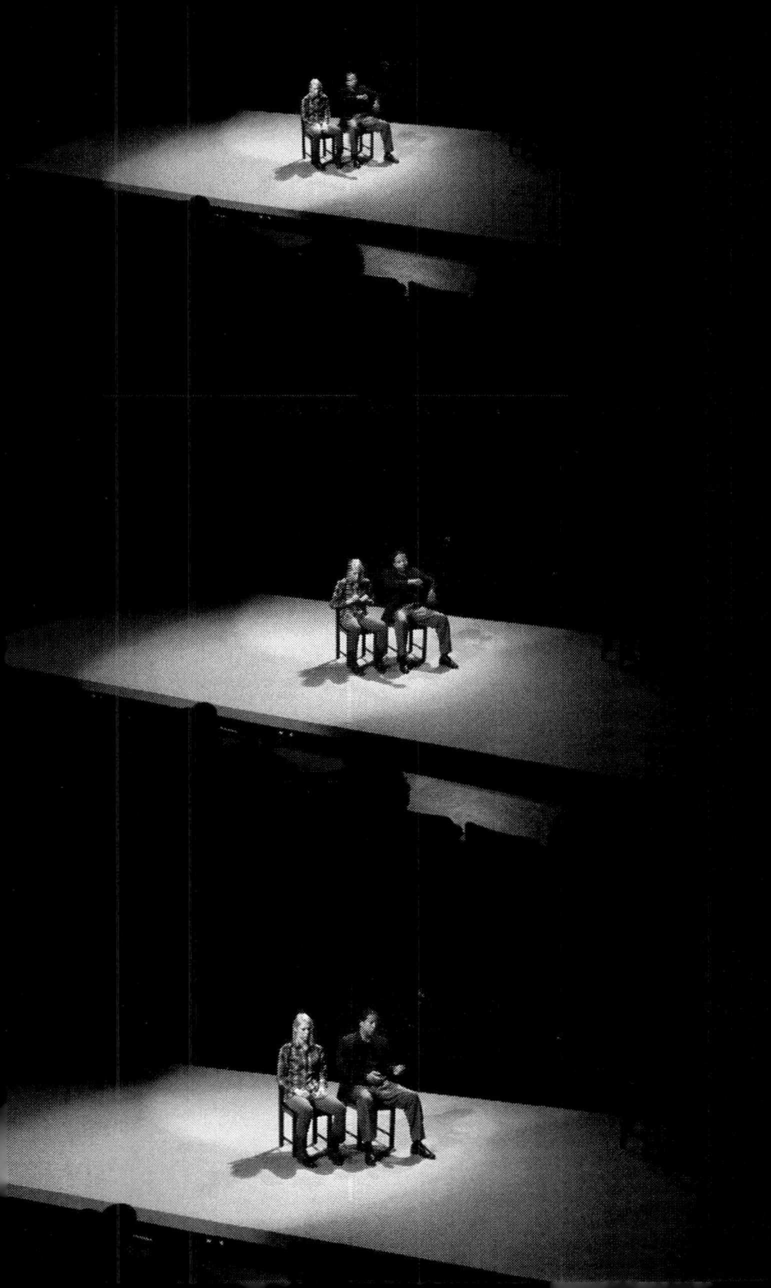

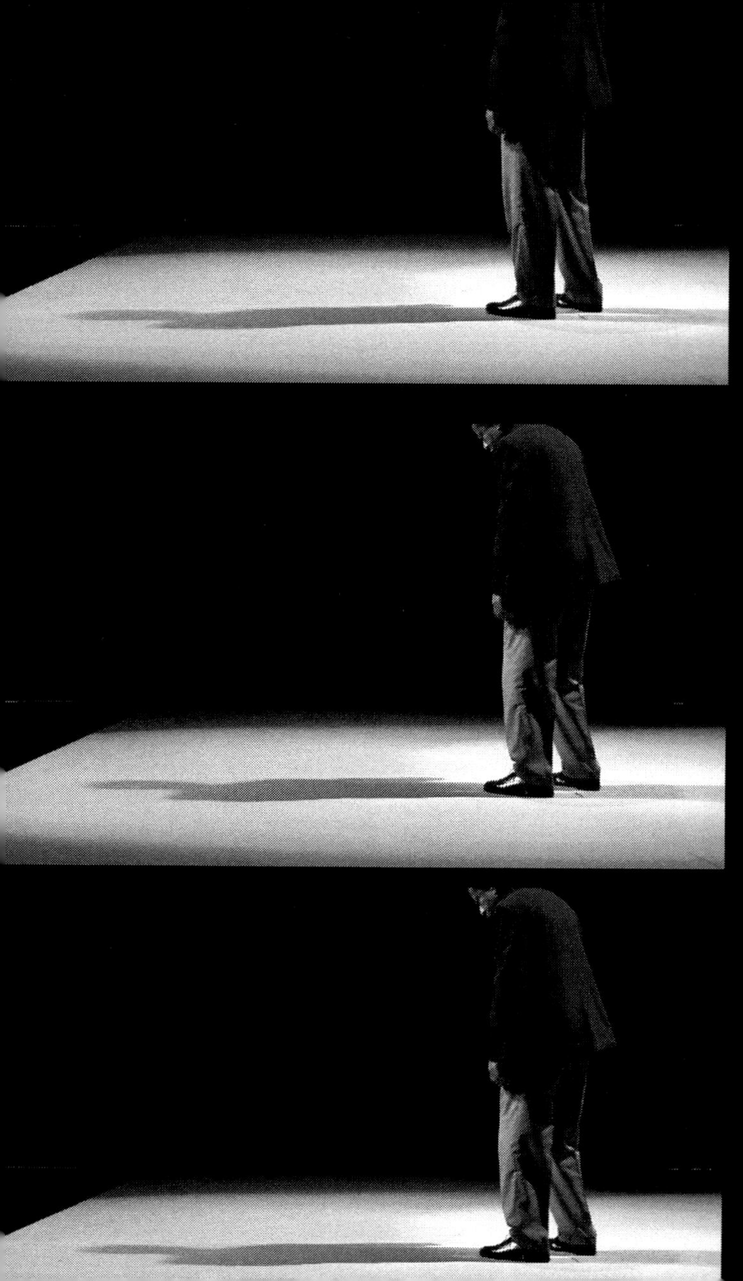

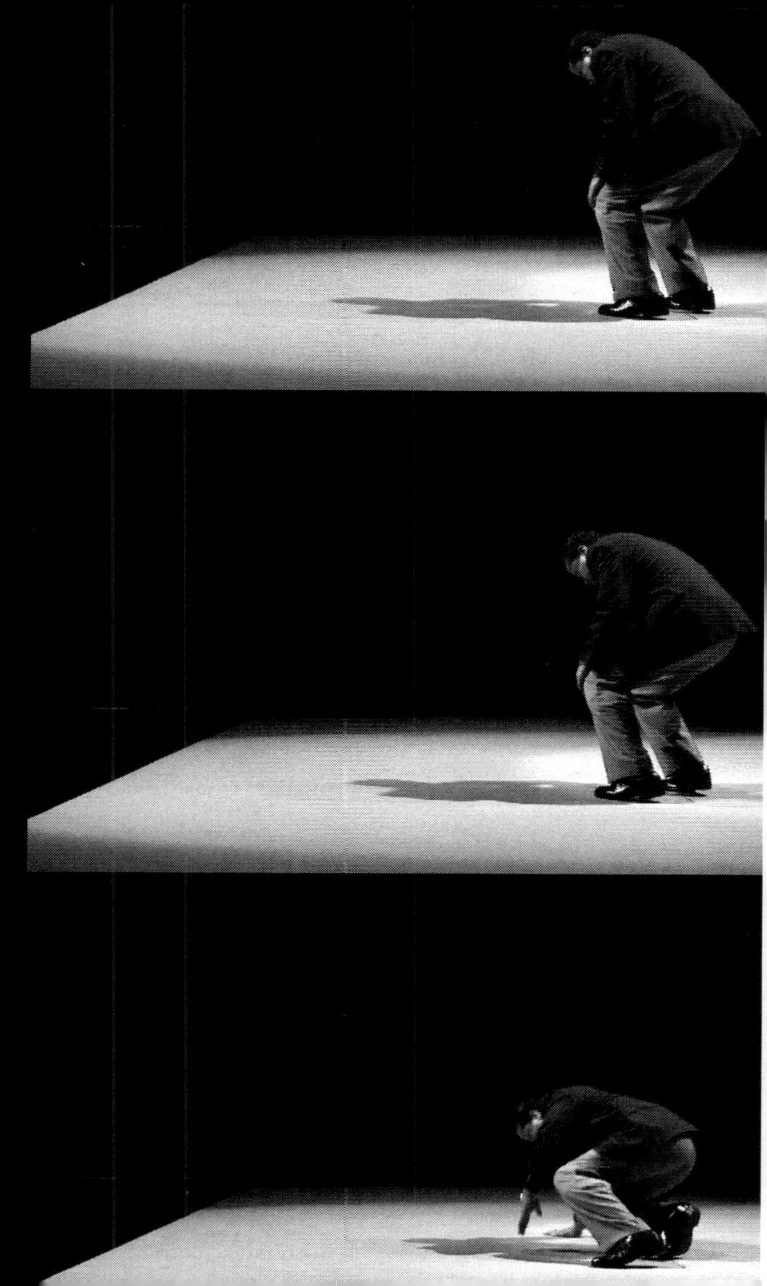

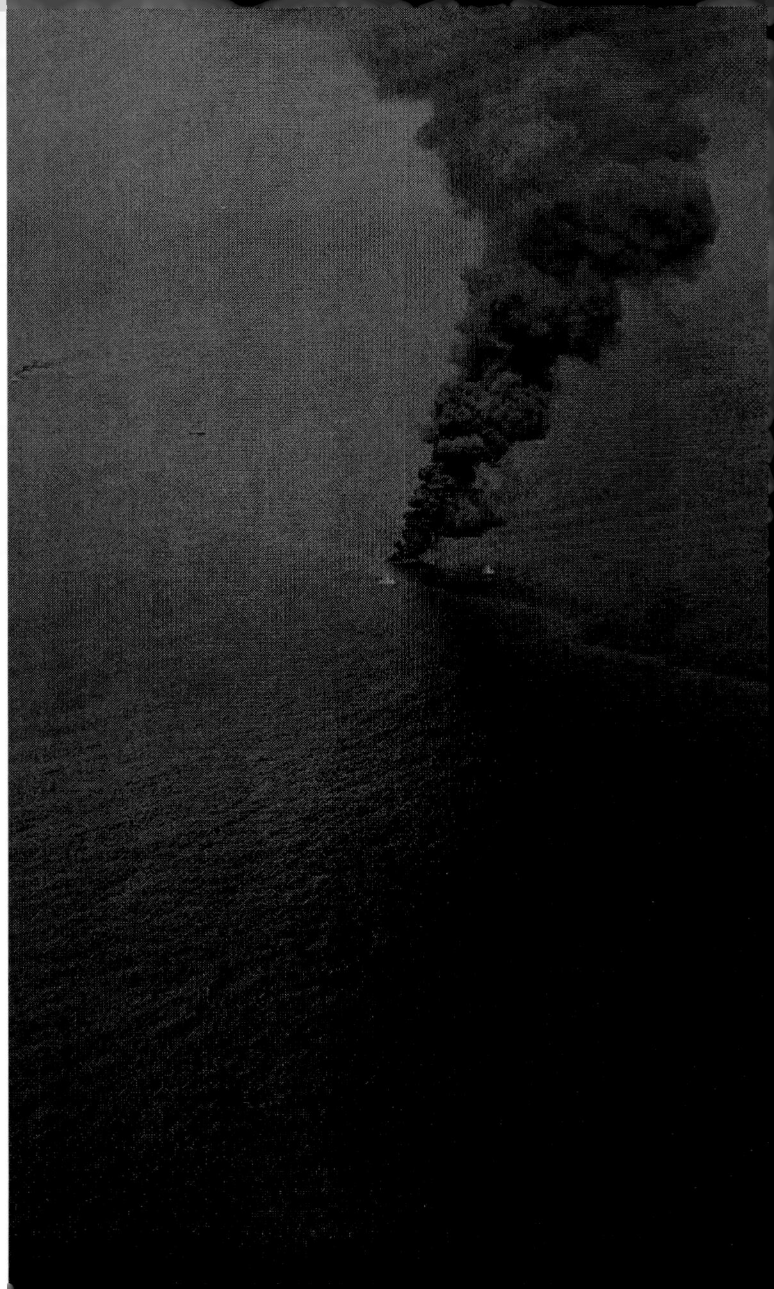

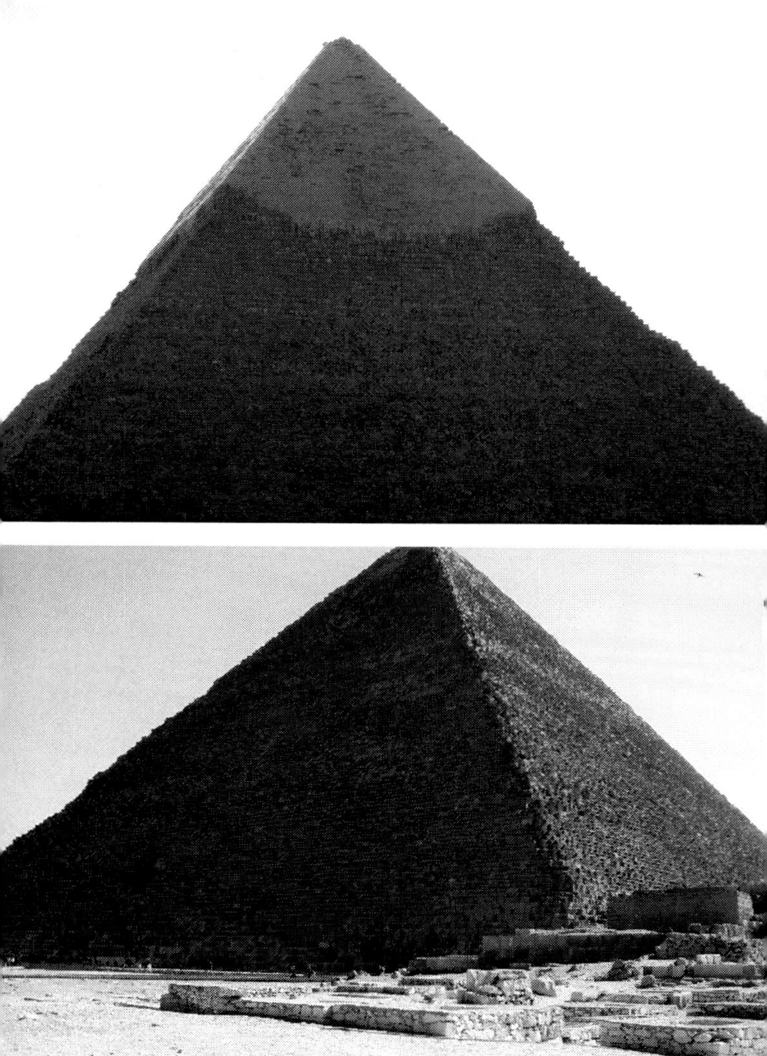

Photographs taken by Amy Patton in Egypt, 2009

Christina Linden

After That You're Sliding in Oil: A Conversation with Amy Patton

Christina Linden: You've mentioned several times over the years your interest in exploring the object-like qualities of narrative or film as something that can be structured and molded like a sculpture. Can you elaborate on that?

Amy Patton: I started making video mostly because I like editing—when you can take something as concrete as a sequence of images and organize it so that it unfolds in a certain way over a period of time; the way you give shape to something that has already happened. Most of the time, the shape emerges from something I see in the original material, so I often find myself writing a totally new script after having shot another kind of film. It's the script the film seems to want once I notice that some other shape is taking over. So rather than sculpting in a concrete way, I see something like a set of images or coincidences I didn't expect and make sense of them or create a frame in which they can exist. It sounds very constructed, but it is also a highly associative process. It's about reading; I think that comes through in the work.

CL: What exactly do you mean by associative process?

AP: I want the things I make to work like thoughts. I've always been interested in how the mind organizes ideas and information. It's an extremely individual and subjective thing, the way we make connections, try to appropriate foreign concepts, or make sense of what we see where there was no sense before. This can be a strange process, and I want to call attention to that strangeness.

CL: The way subjective stories come together and are layered over a film, object, or film-cum-object has a lot to do with perception, but not just yours, right? You leave the experience open; it's not just about what you see but also the contrast between your process and viewers completing the work by making their own connections.

AP: Yes. When it comes to the film work I always feel there are all these different stories going on. I think that contributes to a lot of the contrast, and the openness. The pictures are telling a story, the sound is telling a story, the actors' bodies and voices are telling a story, what they are saying is telling another story, and the way these different elements are framed is another one. The way they come together is a subjective process, and the viewer is part of that.

CL: Let's talk about your new piece in Houston— a kind of theater-in-film scenario. Approaching the screen, viewers enter into the middle of a performance of the play that is simultaneously its own rehearsal. We are guided through it via a meta-structure that extends the interest in voiceover and sound you've also explored in past work. But while these structural

elements that direct narrative experience are not new
for you, the idea of theater is new. This is only the
second time you've worked with professional actors.
Can you talk about how you moved from working
with found footage to writing material for actors, and
your attraction to the idea of filming this material in a
theatre rather than some other kind of setting?

AP: I've worked with actors for only the past year or
so. The element of theater emerged from ideas that are
theatrical to begin with—making connections where
there were none and adapting the staging involved in
exhibiting a work of visual art. Working with actors
draws attention to script and frame. Actors make sense
of a fictional character, inhabiting words that are not
their own to become an invented person. I am interested in this shifting between being something and
performing it, and how this plays out in a particular
setting, in this case a black box theater, the visual
limitations of which were so obvious that I felt I could
tease elements out of it that I could not have in
another scenario. For me, filming theater has to do
with my particular relationship to the image. Actors
are able to make you see things that aren't there,
which is visual in a certain way. The images are all in
your mind. An actor on stage can be sitting on a table,
but if he says, "I'm sitting in a boat," you think, "oh,
he's sitting in a boat," and you see it. It demands an
incredible suspension of disbelief, but it works. I was
also attracted to theater as a form because it was a
blank slate for me. Since I didn't know anything
about it, I felt very free But it's not theater itself that
interests me so much as the idea of the theatrical.

CL: In the end, though, the piece is shown in a museum rather than in the cinema. It's visual art, so it is presented in a specific context. And also vice versa: it's presented in a specific context and so it's visual art. Can you explain what this has to do with the theatrical? The video *Hairpin Magic Wand* and the exhibition *About the object*[1] that we worked on together last year also explored the potential of treating the exhibition space as a kind of stage.

AP: Right, the size of the exhibition space at Blaffer is fairly close to the size of the theater space I worked in, so there is an analogy there. My idea is to project the piece really large, almost floor to ceiling, to imply an extension of the stage into the exhibition space, and to implicate the viewer as a part of the work. In the film you sometimes catch sight of audience members in their seats, which mirrors spectatorship in the museum space. I want viewers in the exhibition to be made aware that something is being performed, not unlike what the audience members within the film are being confronted with. I like to think of the screen as the interface between these two moments of reception.

CL: Which two moments of reception do you mean?

AP: The first moment is when we were in our seats as the audience of the rehearsal, watching the production

1. *Hairpin Magic Wand* was initially produced as an "In Practice" commission by SculptureCenter in Long Island City, New York, and shown at that venue from January 11 to March 22, 2009. It was shown again in the context of the exhibition *About the object*, a thesis exhibition at the Center for Curatorial Studies, Bard College, in Annandale-on-Hudson, New York, on view from April 19 to May 24, 2009.

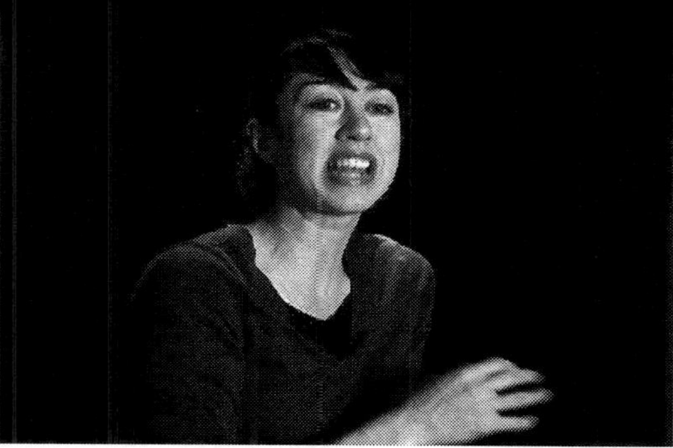

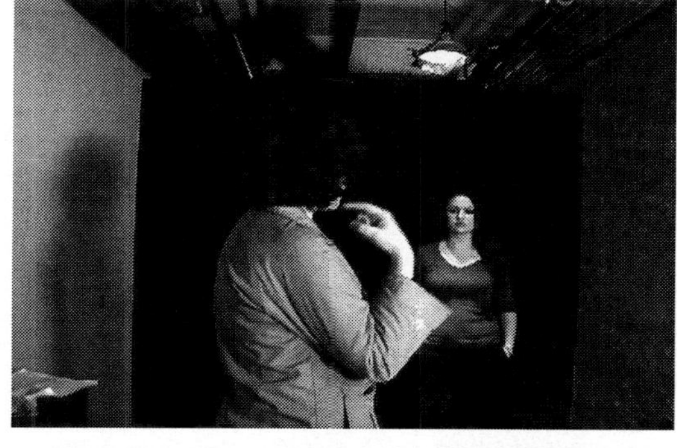

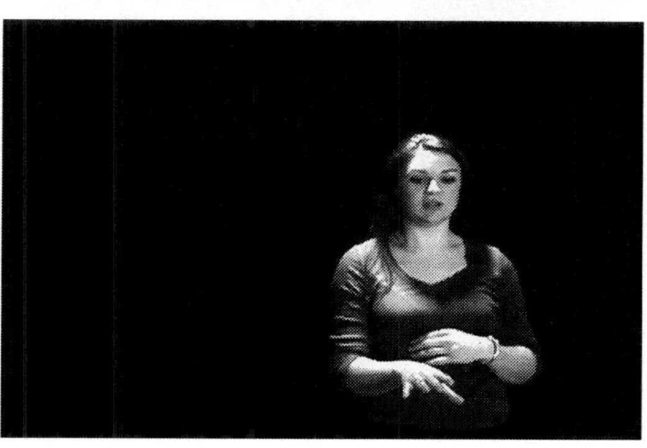

Stills from *Hairpin Magic Wand*, 2009. Video (color, sound), 27:34 min.

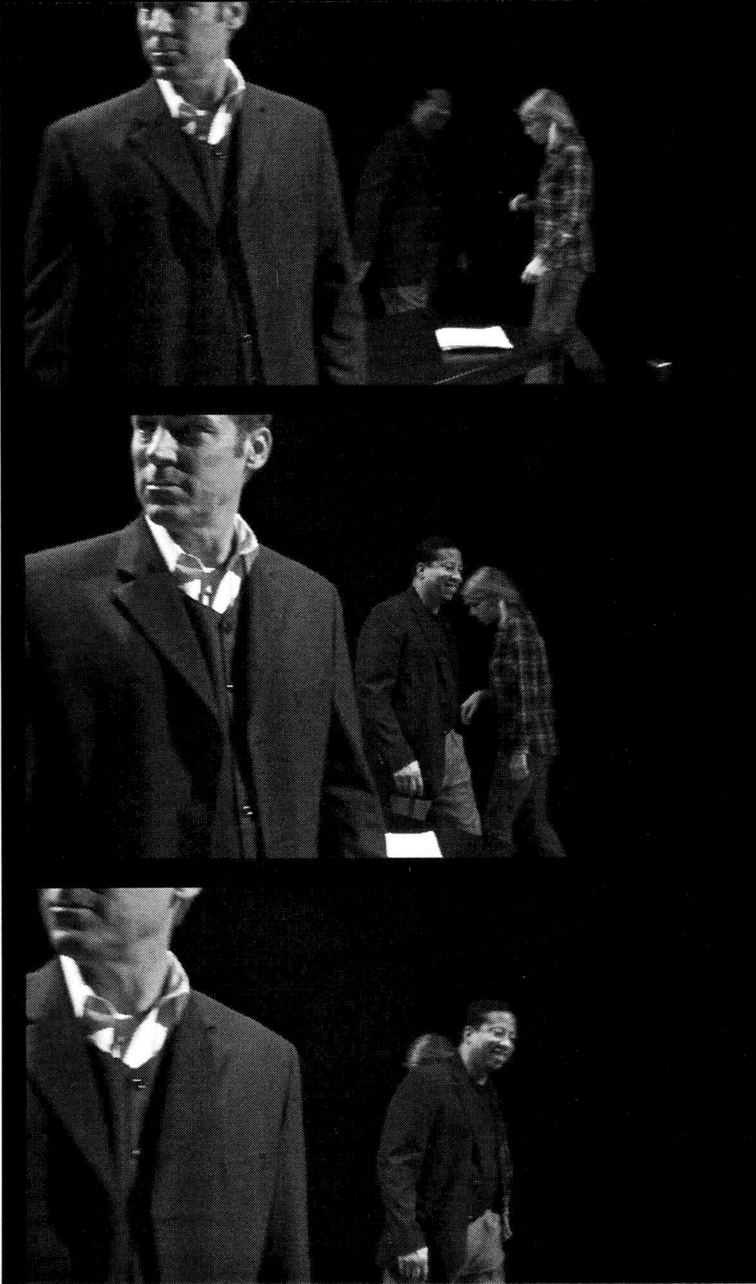

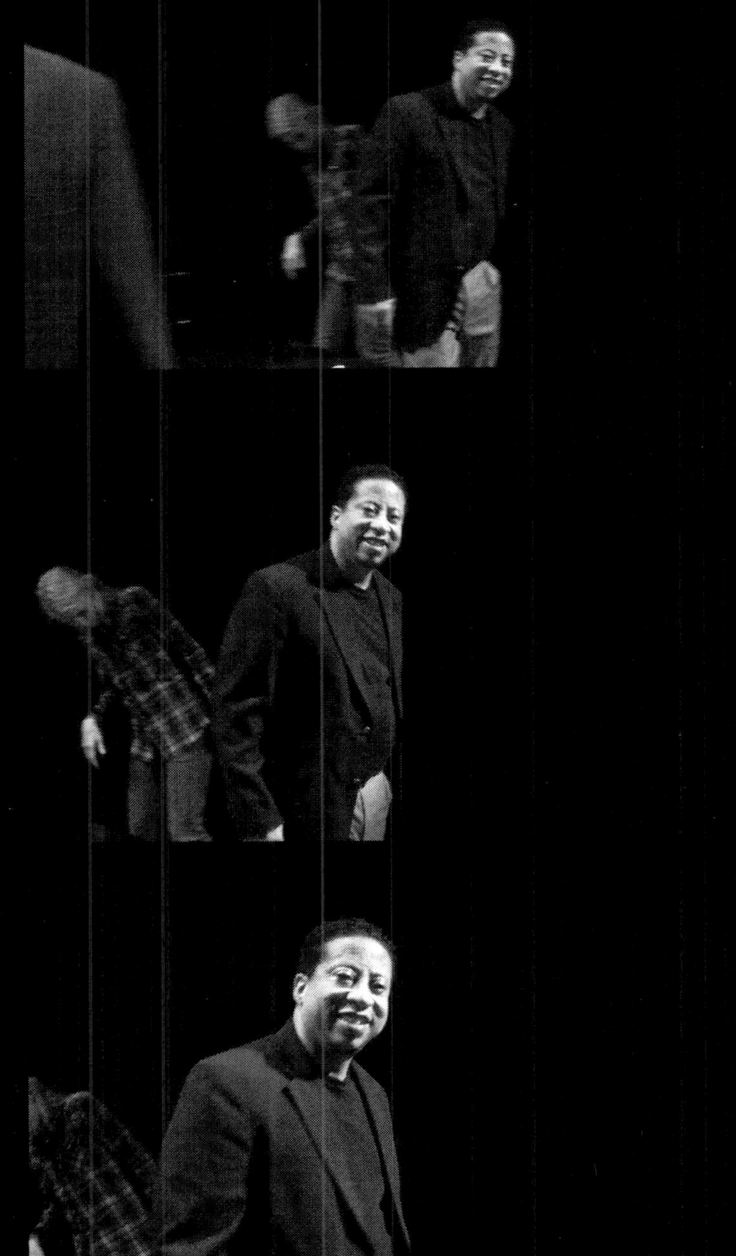

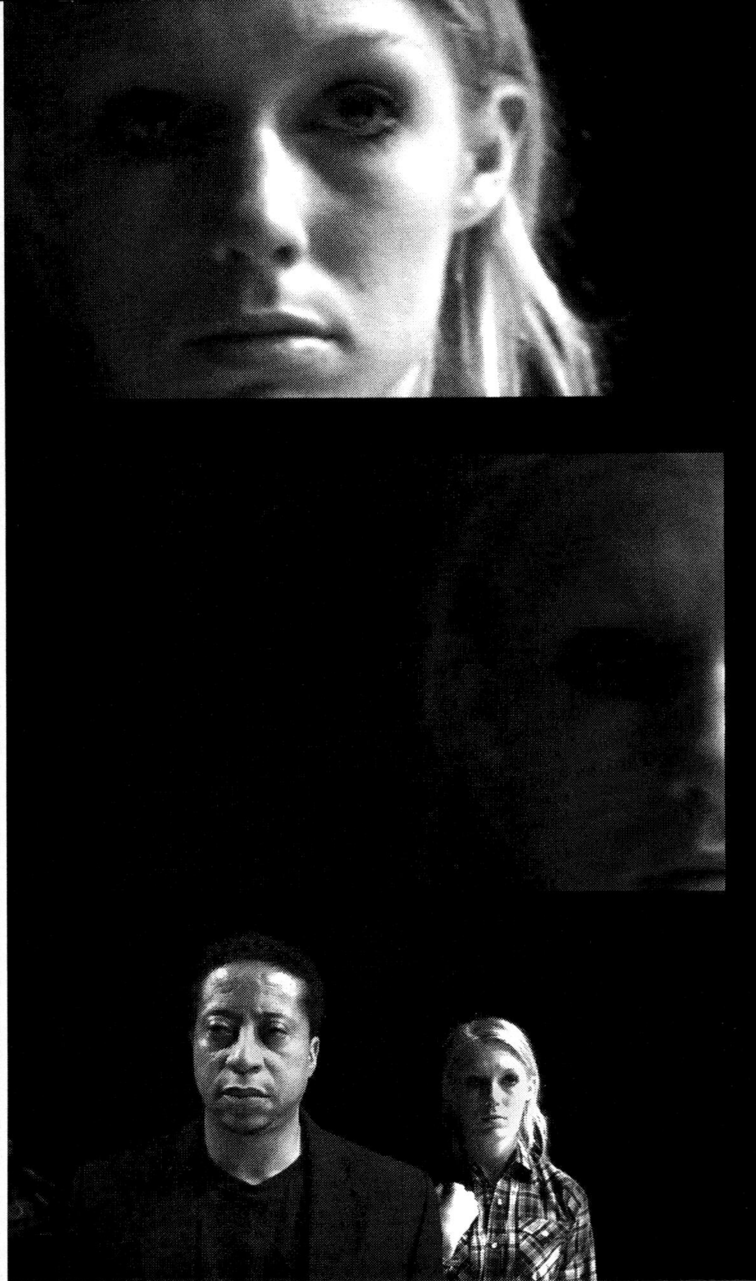

from one perspective. But there was a cameraman trailing the actors at all times, on stage with them, and he was a character himself. The second moment is when someone sees the film, the mediated version of what was seen from the camera's perspective—a completely mobile perspective. Something remarkable about the production process was how quiet it was. The actors didn't use their theater voices, so sitting in the audience you had to listen really closely to what they were saying. On the film, of course, it all seems quite normal.

CL: This piece, written based on "found" text from Upton Sinclair's 1927 novel *Oil!*, is not the first instance in which literature has been an important reference for you. What role has literature played in your thinking and work?

AP: I get a lot of inspiration from literary sources— but usually less in terms of content than in the way different perspectives are embodied. In terms of authors, Nabokov and Borges have been important influences.[2] Nabokov because of his images and their appeal to the senses, but also because his language is so precise— every word has a kind of gravity. And of course the labyrinthine quality of Borges's work appeals to me very much. I'm really interested in this idea of creating symmetries and he is all about systems, shifts and mirrors, which he presents in a really compact form. He was also a miniaturist, and that economy appeals to me—not needing an entire novel to develop a story.

2. Vladimir Nabokov (1899–1977), Russian-American novelist and short-story writer, and Jorge Luis Borges (1899–1986), Argentinian essayist, poet, and writer.

This is one reason I make short films and videos rather than long cinematic works.

CL: Speaking of cinema, parts of Sinclair's *Oil!* also inspired the script for Paul Thomas Anderson's 2007 mainstream film *There Will Be Blood.* But your work remains much closer to Sinclair's socialist concerns, at least in outline. The central tension in Anderson's movie develops between the forces of (relatively corrupt) religion and (totally corrupt) capitalism. But while the character of H.W. Plainview in Anderson's film goes against his father's wishes by moving away to found a rival oil drilling company, your main character, Bunny, gets involved with leftist labor activists and sets out to "understand the working people" by becoming a laborer herself. I know you had Anderson's film in mind when you made the work—what was its significance for you?

AP: *There Will Be Blood* is such a radical departure from Sinclair's book as to be pretty much unrecognizable. It totally changes the storyline, adding several new characters and major dramatic elements that don't exist at all in the original. Also, the film—which I like very much, by the way—deals with only the first hundred and fifty pages of the novel. Although I excerpt text from the same section, I am ultimately more interested in the remaining two-thirds of the book, which has a very clear and strong socialist agenda, as you mention. Sinclair believed that literature would change the world, and his work actually did cause sweeping reform in a way that seems unfathomable today. It was a massive bestseller in its time, and you can tell that it was written for mass consumption.

While Anderson's characters are richly complicated, conflicted souls, Sinclair's characters are papery, more like puppets illustrating principles. It is a political parable. In the play in my film, I follow Sinclair's story much more closely than Anderson did, in part to examine its call-to-revolution aspect and consider how it might relate today—if it were even possible. I was interested in the book as a historical snapshot, and for the strangeness of the language as it comes out of contemporary characters' mouths.

CL: Not long before Upton Sinclair wrote *Oil!*, Bertolt Brecht based his play *Jungle of Cities* [written 1921–24] partly on Sinclair's best-known early work, The Jungle [1906]. The possibilities for literature, theater, and art to reflect or embody leftist politics were a major concern in the 1920s, and the major concern for what I see as two of the primary influences for your film. In fact, the introduction of Brechtian distancing techniques in your work is something else that makes it anti–*There Will Be Blood*, in political terms at least. Do you agree with that assessment?

AP: No. I think of it more as a return to the original material—trying to figure out what it was about—than a critique of Hollywood film (though I am very interested in the way we use Hollywood to reconstruct history). Anderson and I explore different parts of the same thing, and I am interested in what he's left out and why. A lot of the material he omits feels weird and outdated now—contemporary audiences would have no connection to seventy percent of the story, and I am interested in that disconnect, among other things.

CL: I would say that many of the elements in Sinclair's novel still do resonate strongly today, though. The story is built around characters negotiating ideas of profit, capitalism, corporate domination, religious zealotry…. Can we talk a bit more about the political implications of Sinclair's original material but also of your project, and of taking on this subject matter in Texas? Obviously, oil is a very politically charged topic in general, and you deliberately filmed the piece in Houston, an important base for U.S. oil production and one of the largest oil-based economies in the world.

AP: I certainly had this in mind, and my interest in reviving Sinclair's content has a lot to do with what I see as its continued relevance. I wanted to draw attention to the current political and social implications of these issues—and how we have changed the way we think about them. I'm interested in that period of social organization, labor unions, and leftist activity. At the same time the film is meant to show a disconnect, mediating material from a now dusty-seeming time in American history and trying to understand what it means today, why it seems dusty, and why we don't really think of it any more. The play within a film shows a slippage between a staged rehearsal situation and the constructed cinematic one. I couldn't have made the piece in Berlin, because it had to be staged and then shown in the place where it would resonate. I am originally from Texas, so the site has a strong personal resonance for me as well. I feel a strong connection to the place, the actors, and the audience.

CL: Can you say something about Bunny, your protagonist?

AP: In Sinclair's novel, a man nicknamed Bunny is
the main character, an idealist negotiating what he sees
as the evils of greed and capitalism embodied by his
oil-tycoon father. We follow Bunny as he comes into his
own, building his virtue through exposure to radical
ideas in college and becoming involved in the union
activity at his dad's company. For me, this character has
a lot to do with the idea of building a kind of identity.
Directing actors is an interesting way to think about
identity in relation to role-playing, and I wanted to
emphasize this. When my Bunny tells her father that
she's going away to become a worker, for example,
the film feels like a rehearsal situation. It's ambiguous.
As she reads her lines, the whole thing sounds like a
rehearsal, but at the same time it is choreographed—
and photographed. This creates a distance from the
material. I wanted to draw attention to what was being
said rather than to the character saying it.

CL: So at that moment she is a mouthpiece for something
else, both as an actor and as a character.

AP: Absolutely. The character in the book also functions
as a mouthpiece for Sinclair to express his opinions as a
serious and very devoted activist. That is the language
I wanted to activate.

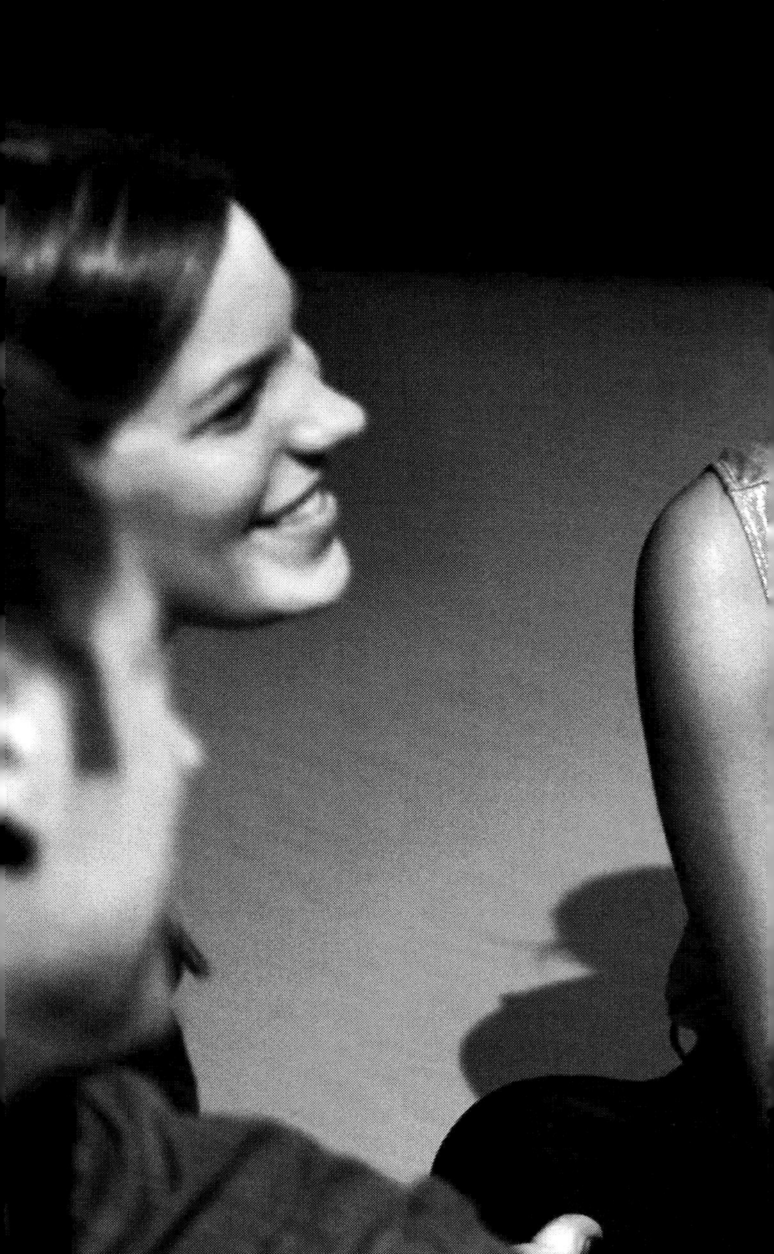

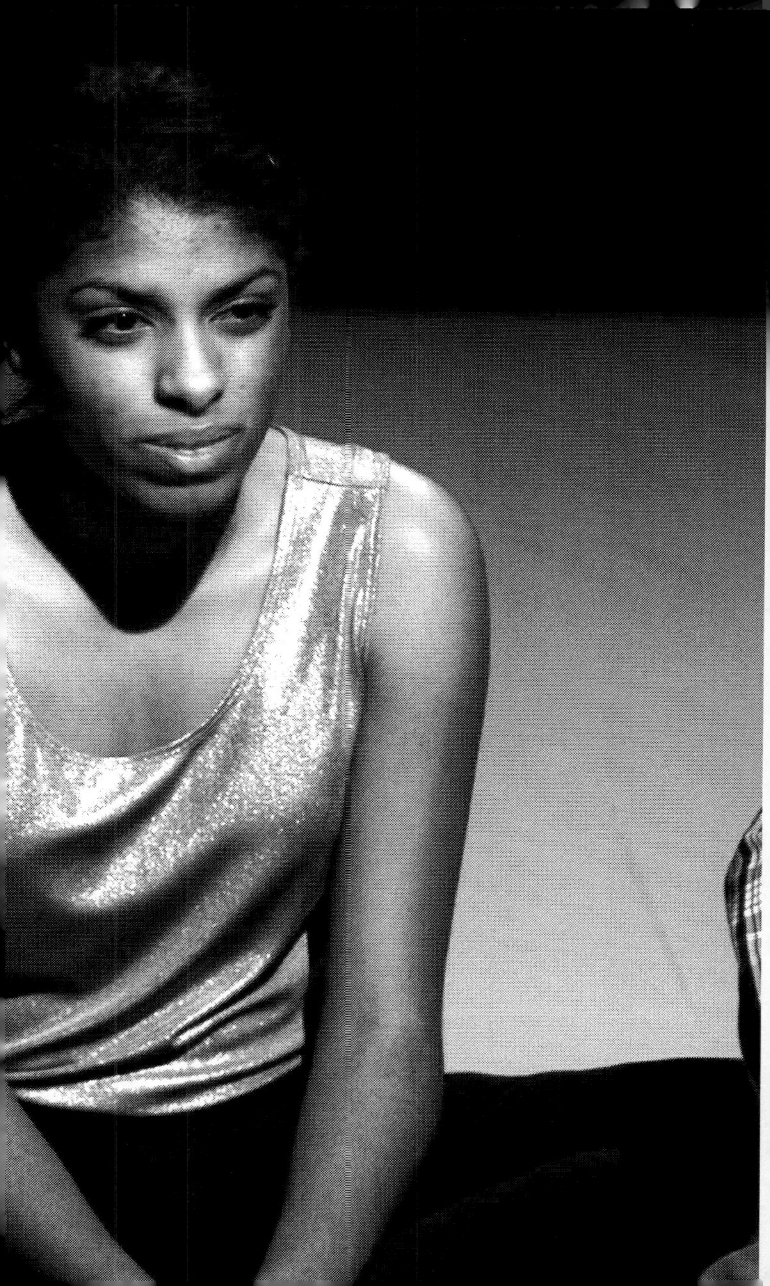

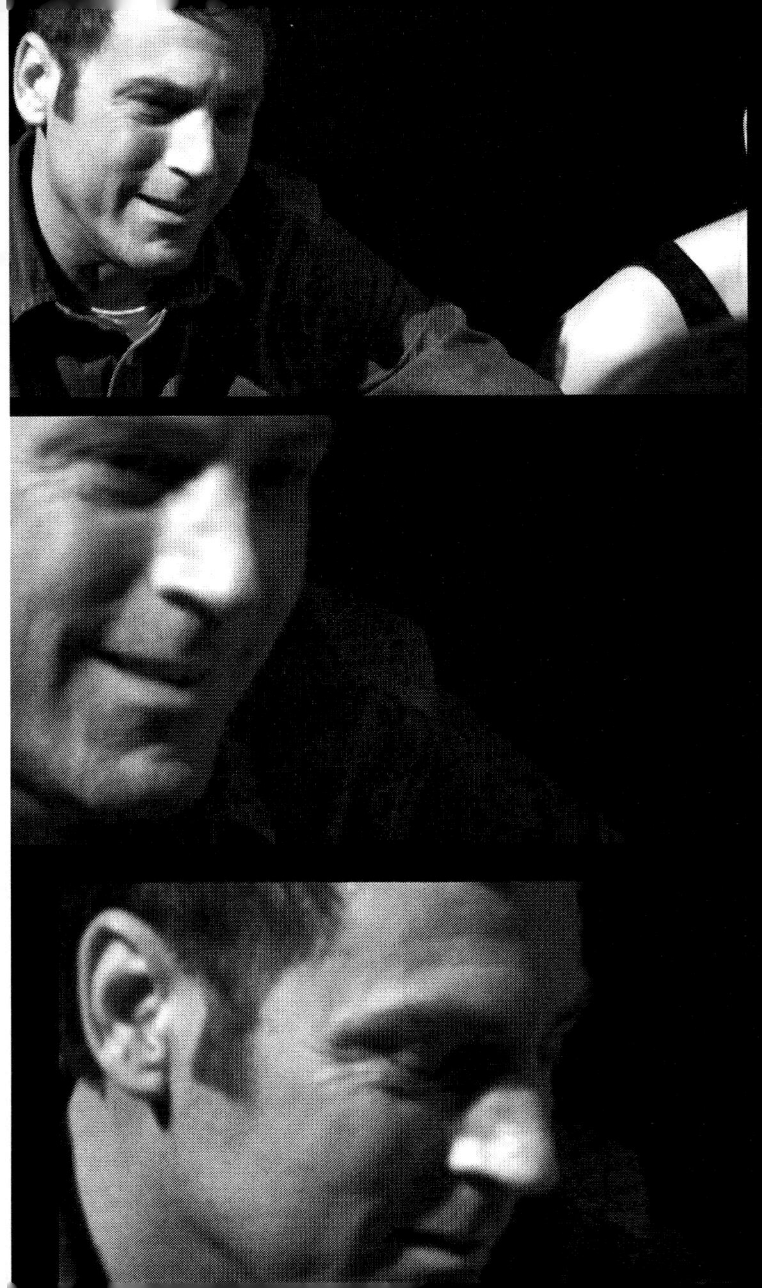

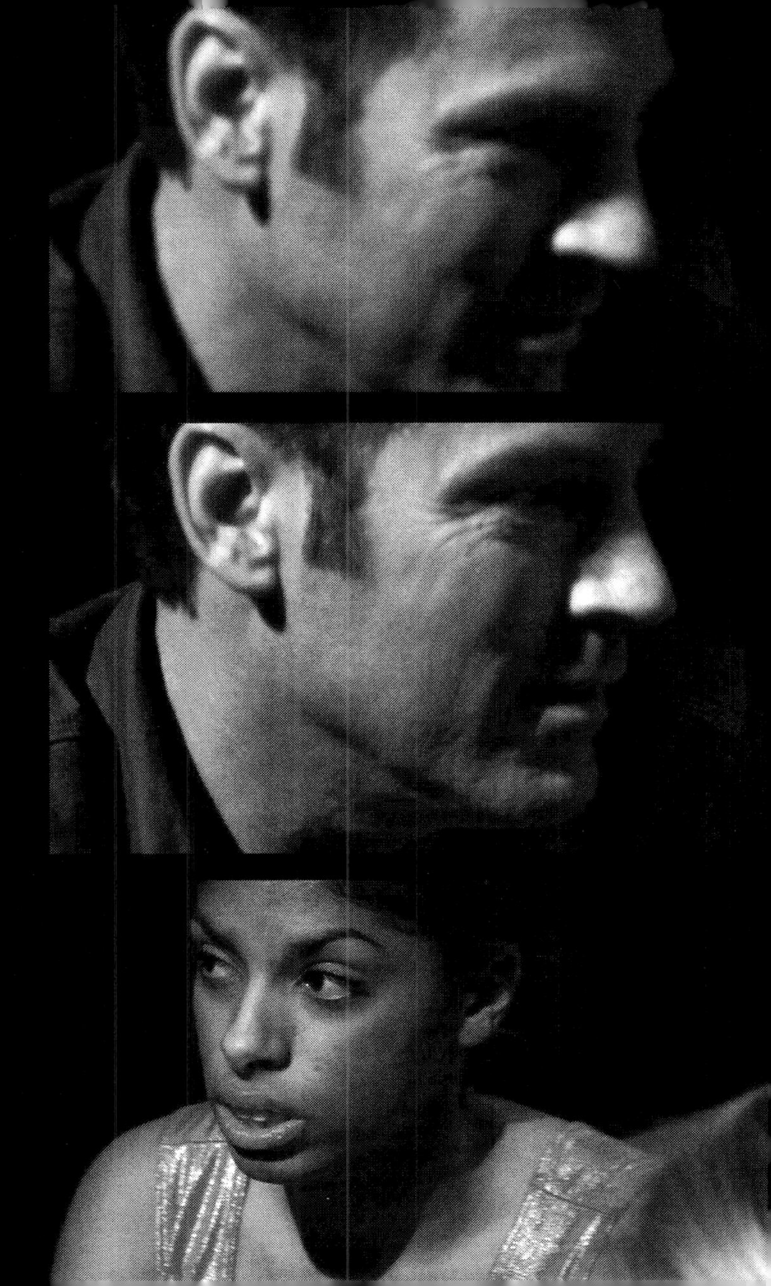

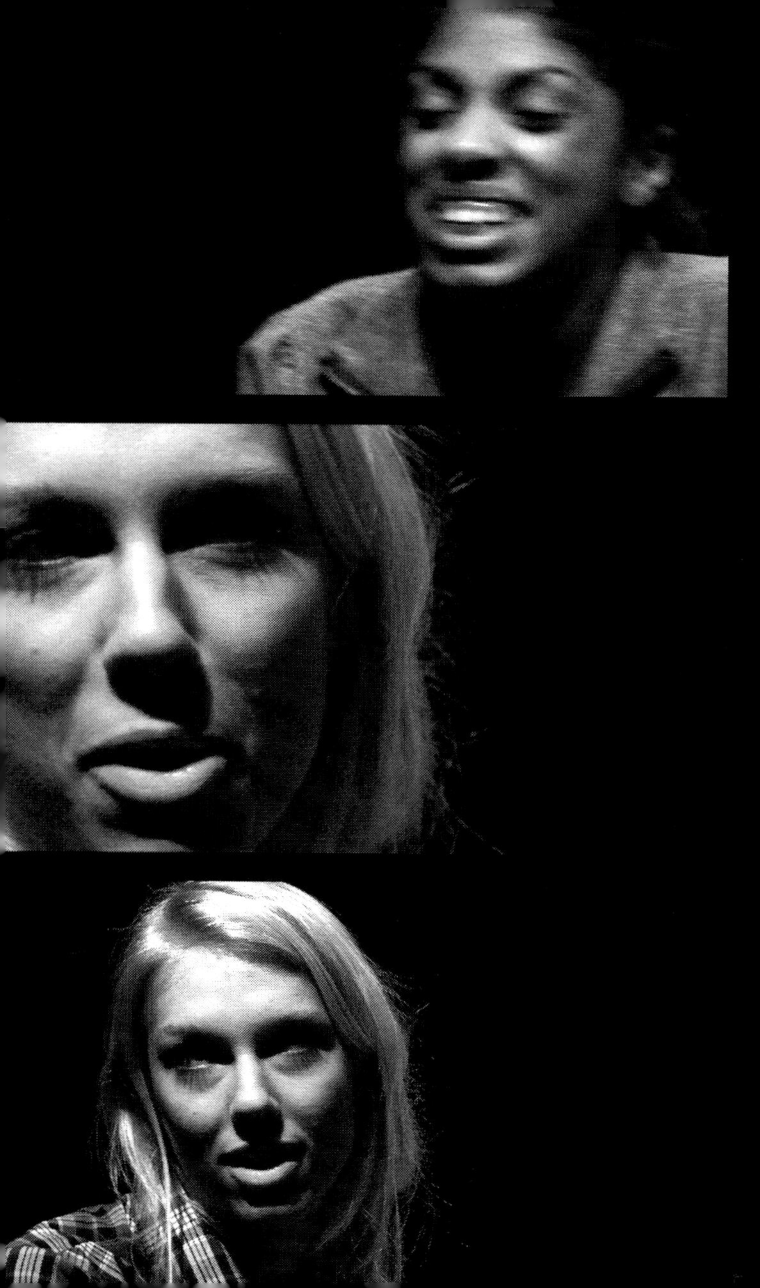

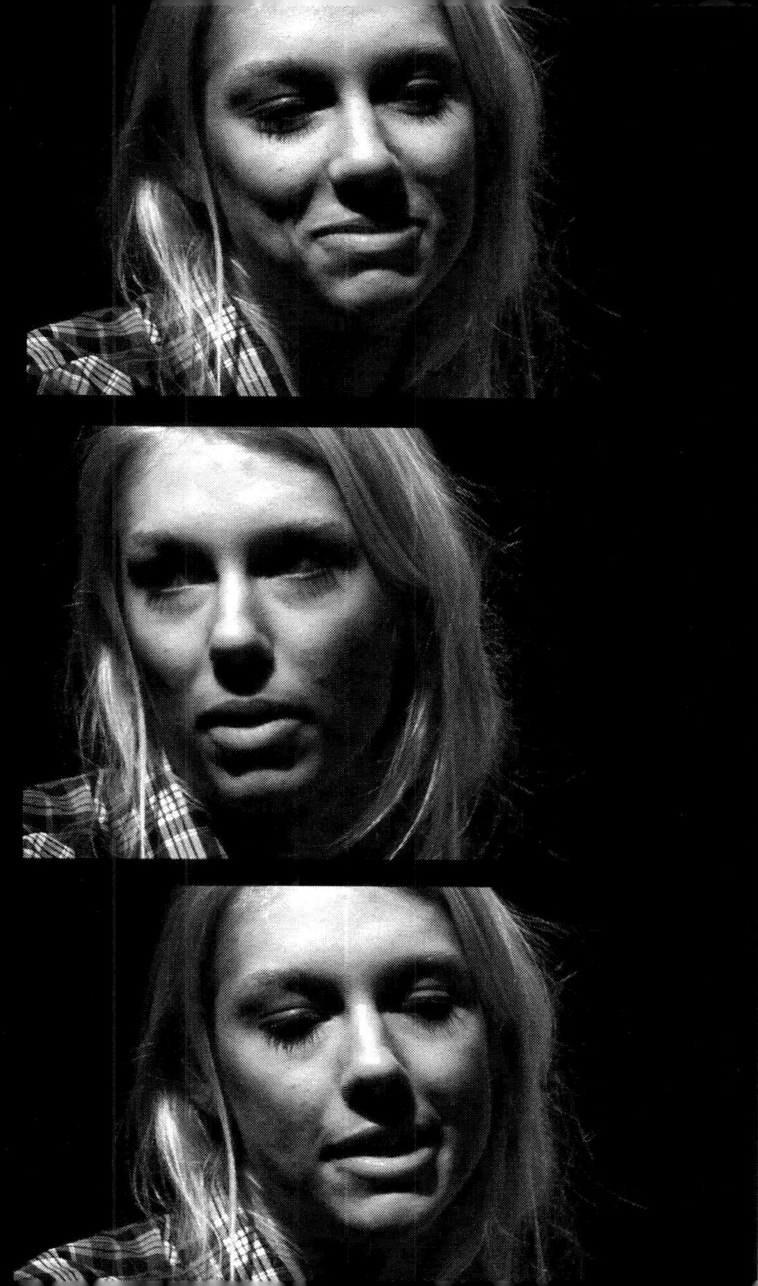

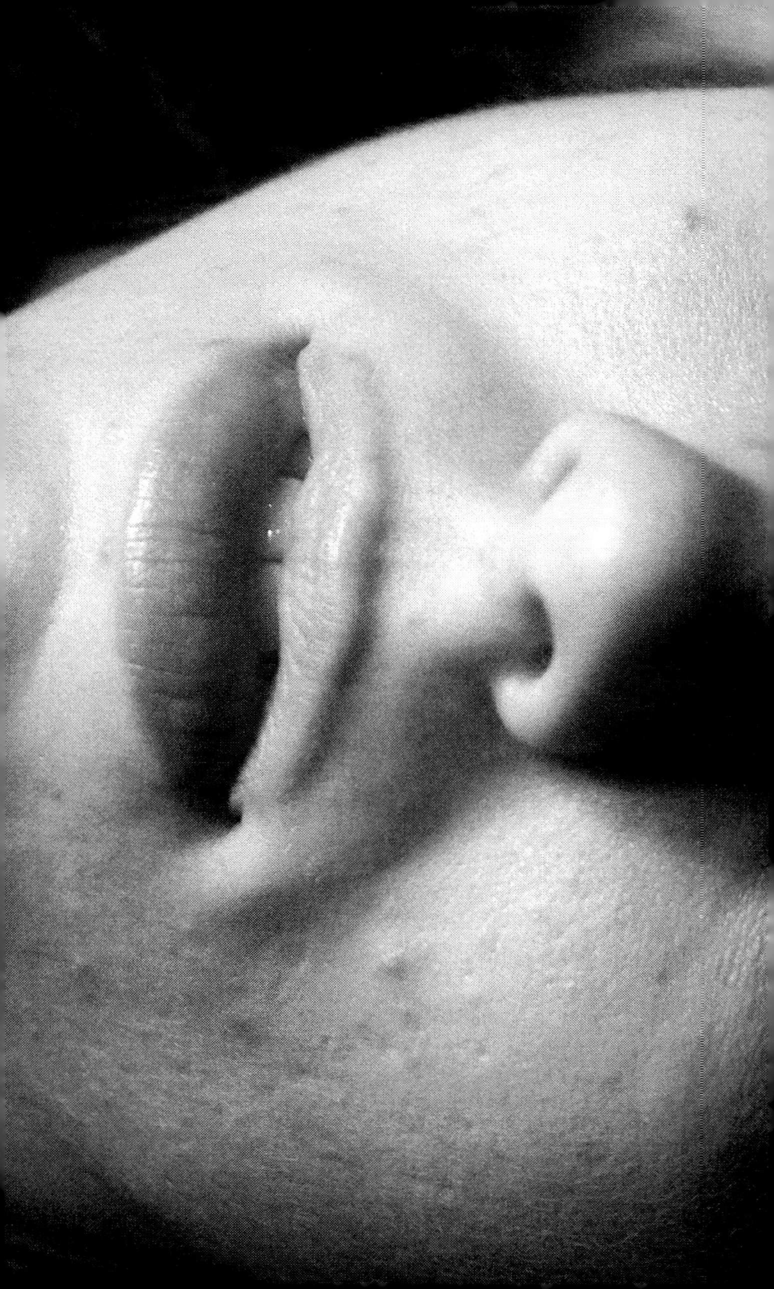

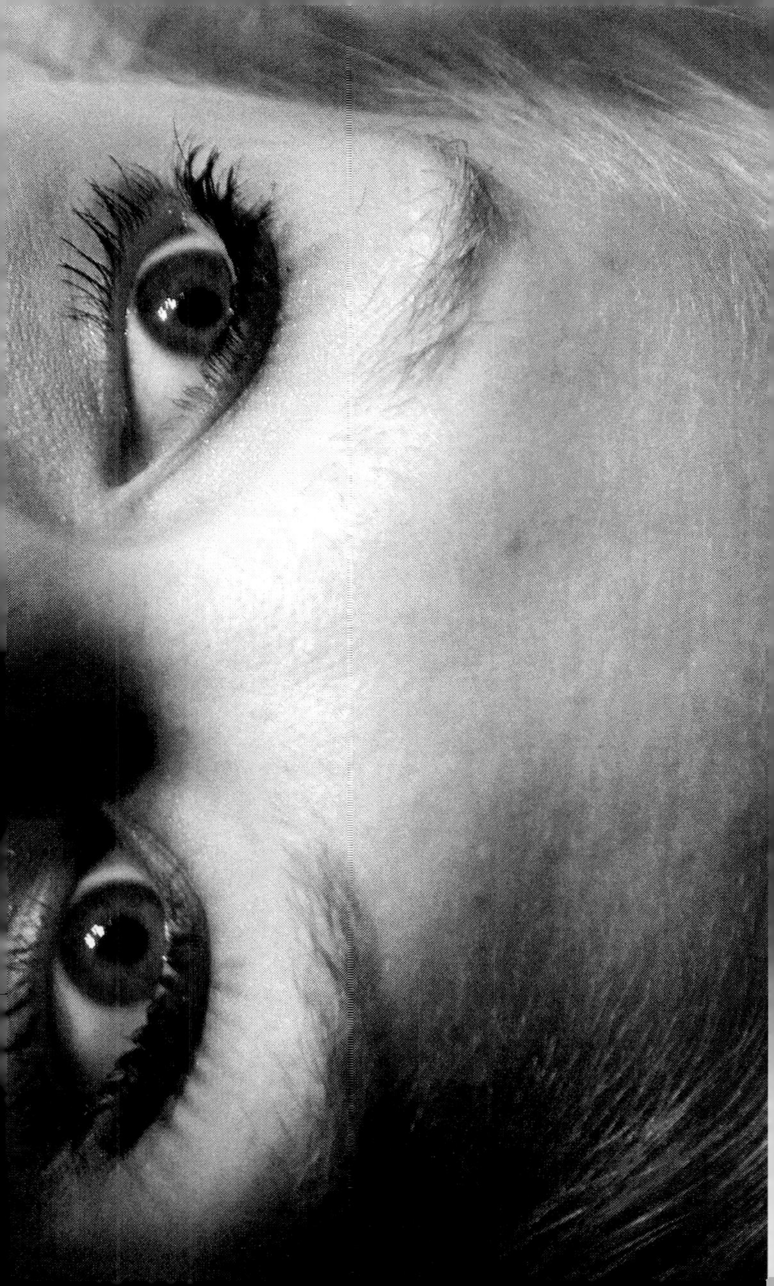

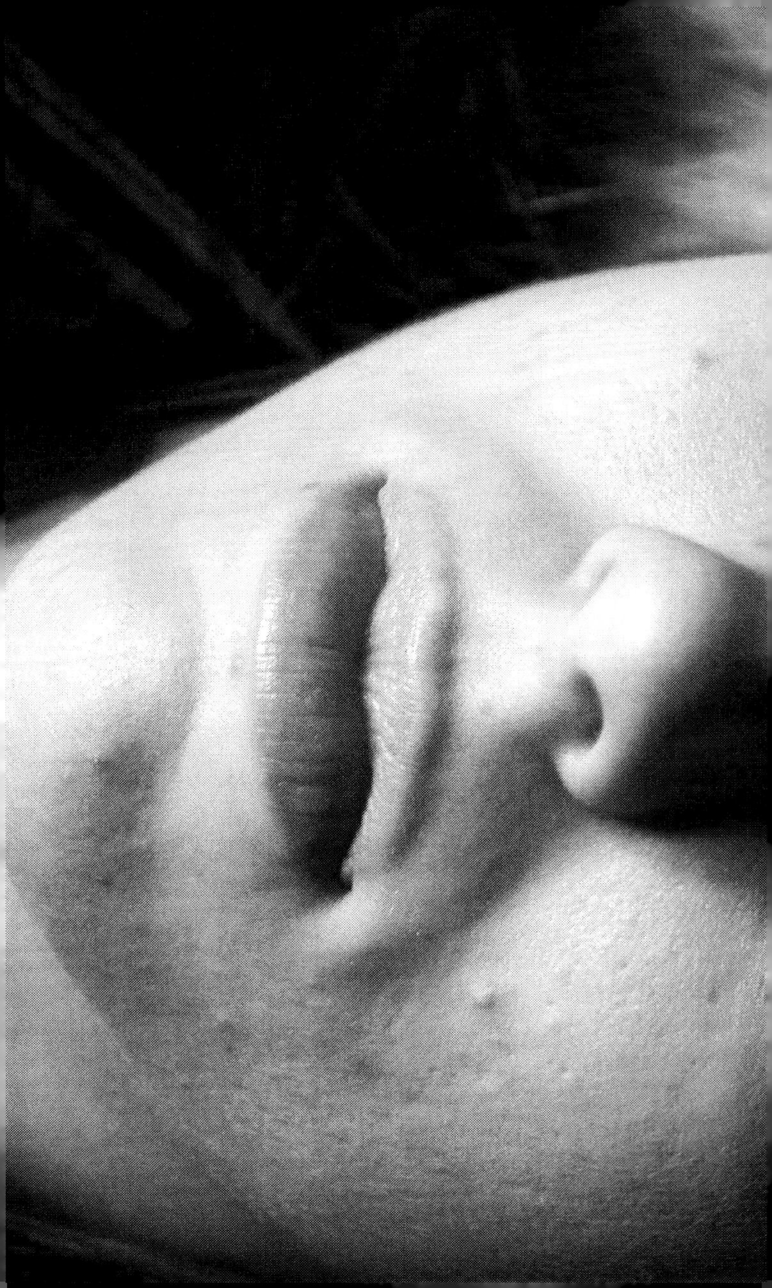

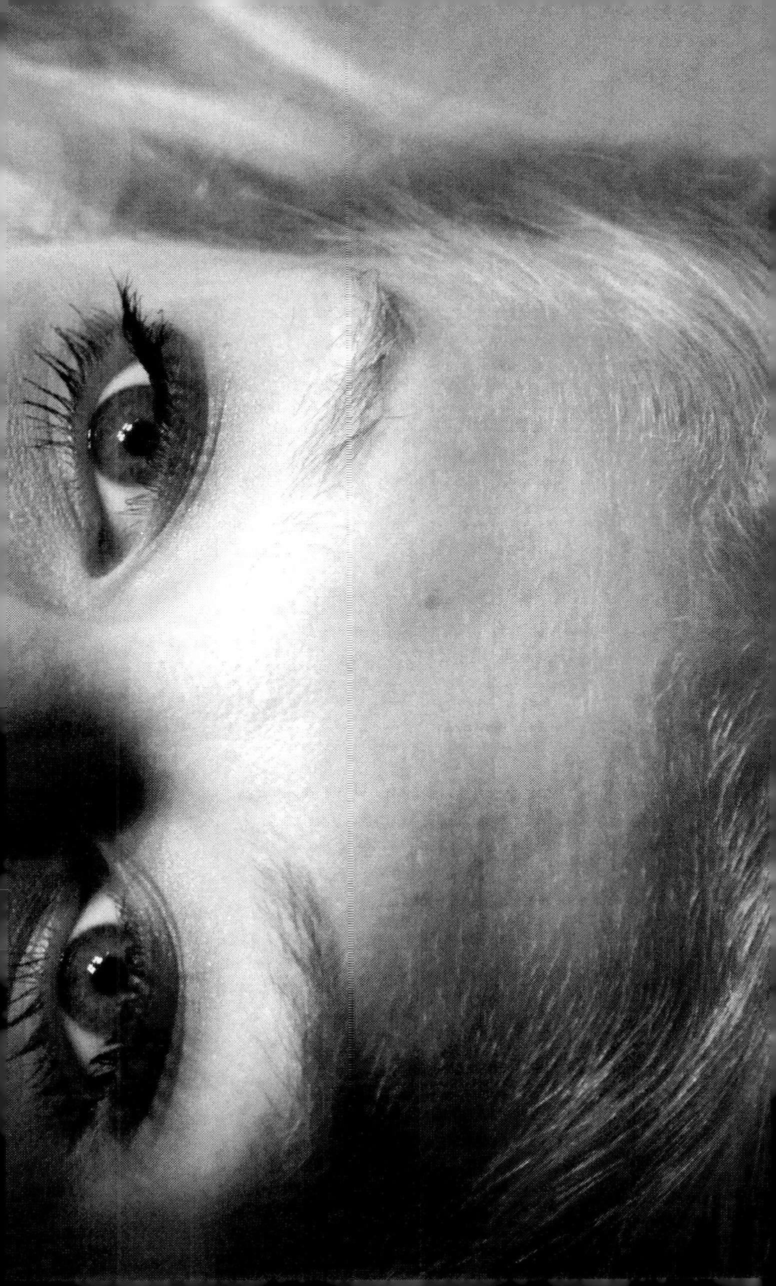

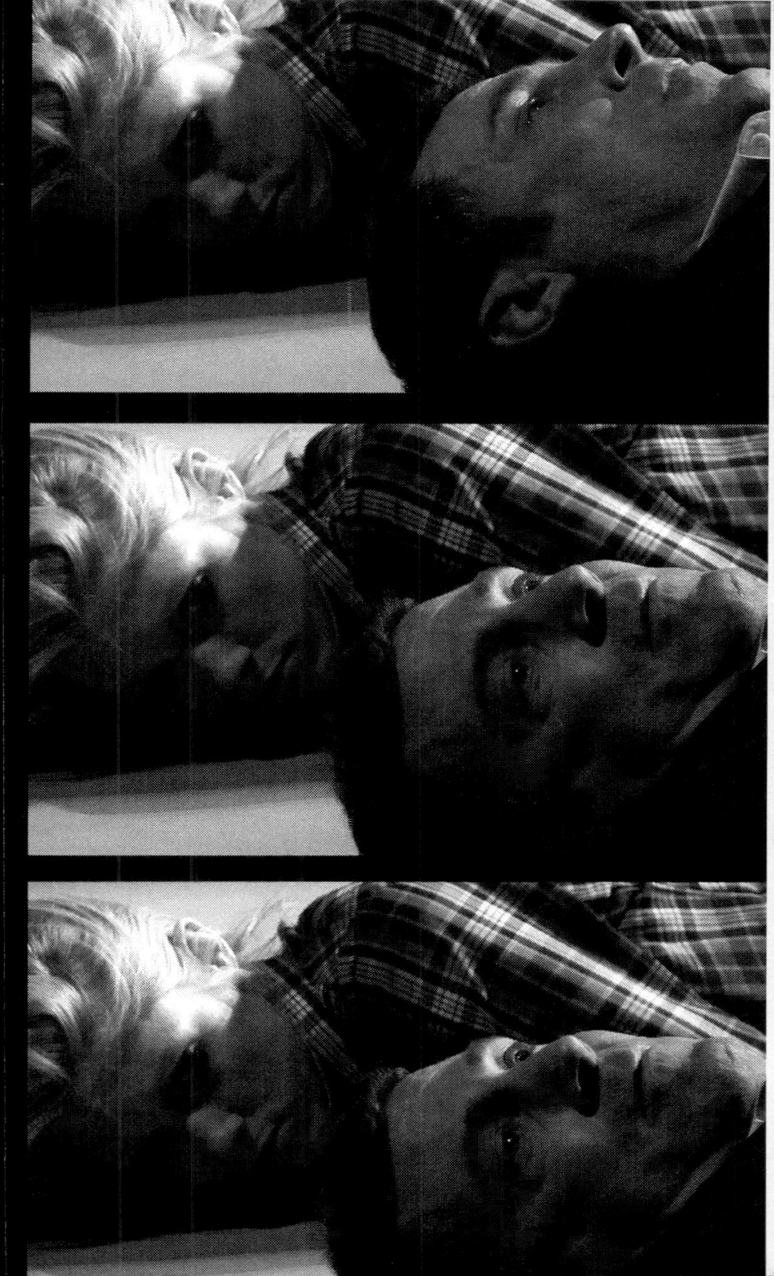

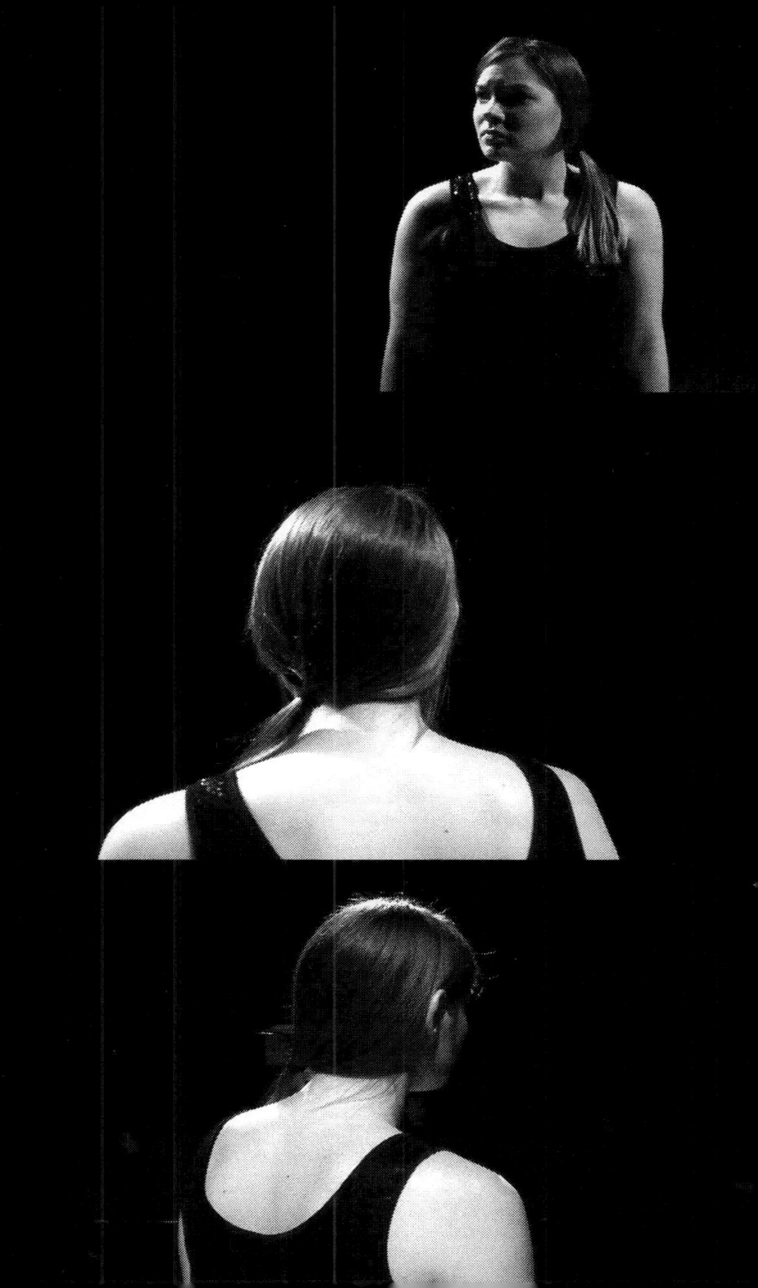

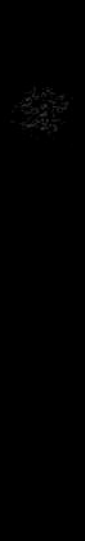
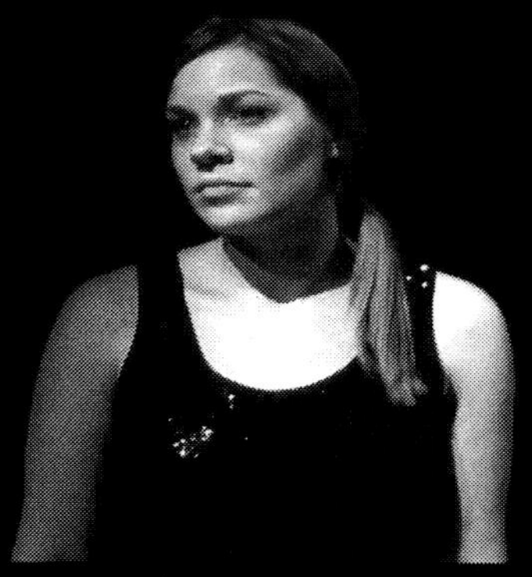
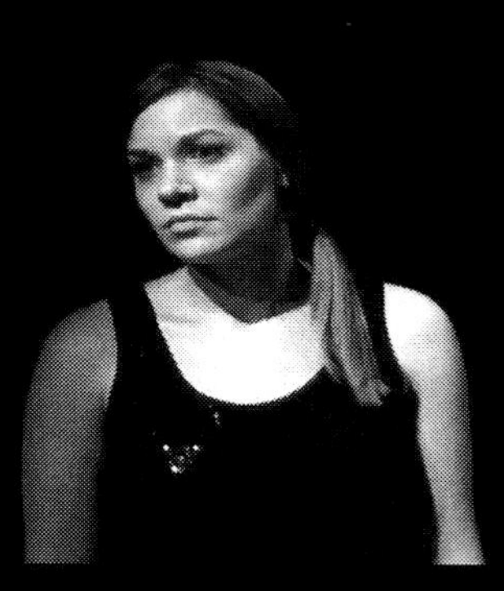
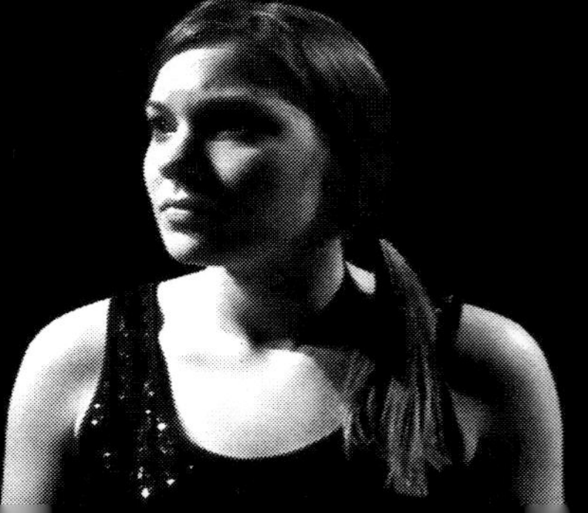

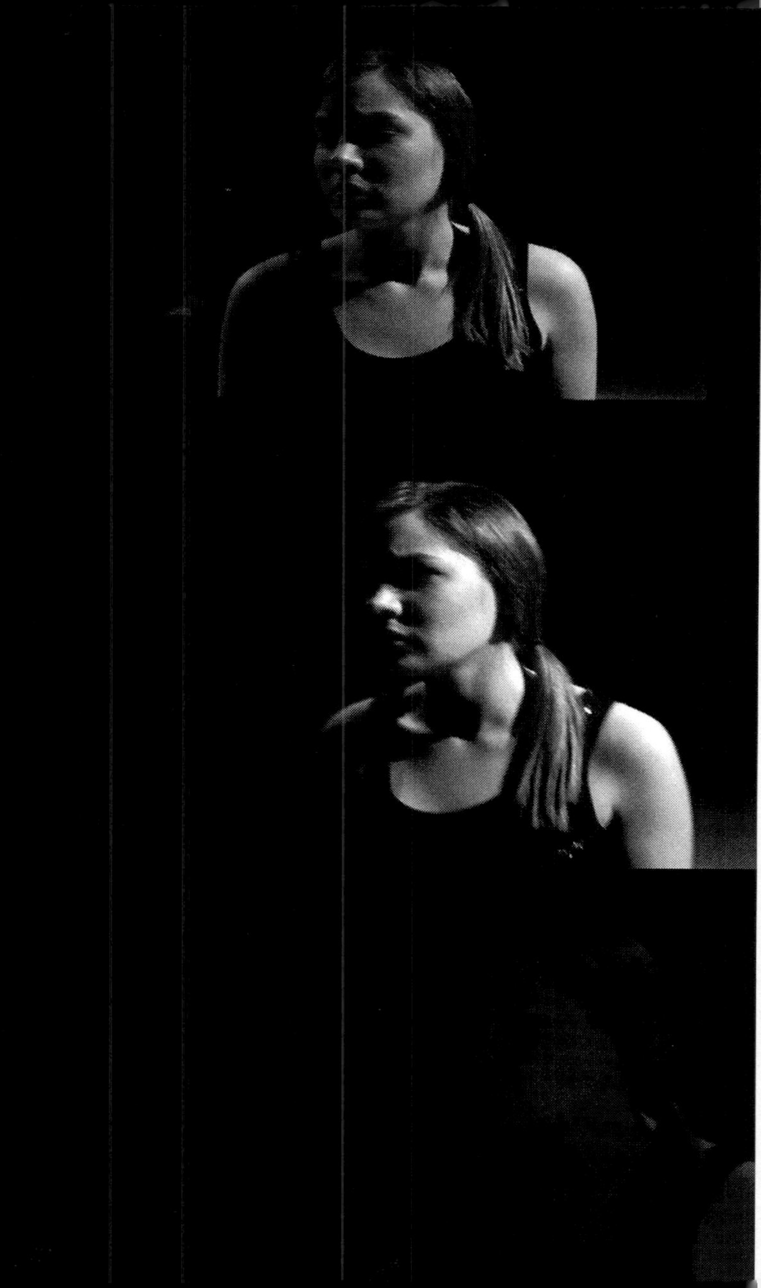

ARTIST'S BIOGRAPHY

Born 1979, Nacogdoches, Texas
Lives and works in Berlin, Germany

EDUCATION
2005 MFA, Experimental Media Design, Universität der Künste,
Berlin, Germany
2000 BFA and BA, University of Texas, Austin, Texas

SELECTED EXHIBITIONS AND SCREENINGS
2010 *Noir Complex—City, Story, Destruction & Death*, Magazin 4,
Bregenzer Kunstverein, Bregenz, Germany, May 29–August 22
2009 *Zeigen: An Audio Tour Through Berlin by Karin Sander*,
Temporäre Kunsthalle Berlin, December 5–January 10, 2010
Reihe Experimentalfilm, D21 Kunstraum, Leipzig, Germany,
October 1 (screening)
Fragmented Series of Movements, SE8, London, September
26–27 (screening)
Amy Patton, EXHIBITION, New York, April 20–21 (solo)
About the object, Spring Exhibitions and Projects, Series 2,
Bard College, Center for Curatorial Studies and Hessel
Museum of Art, Annandale-on-Hudson, New York,
April 19–May 24 (solo)
In Practice Winter '09, SculptureCenter, Long Island City,
New York, January 11–March 22
2008 *Detour*, Third International Film Festival, Cairo, Egypt,
November 30 (screening)
THISISCURATING 1–40, with Mario Pfeifer, Firstdraft
Gallery, Surry Hills, New South Wales, Australia, April 23–
May 10
The More Things Change . . ., 5th Bangkok Experimental
Film Festival (BEFF 5), Thailand, March 25–30 (screening)
2007 *Notes on Places*, Kunsthalle Berlin-Lichtenberg, Germany,
November 5 (screening)
My Own Story, KunstFilmBiennale, Cologne, Germany,
October 18–24 (screening)
Kronacher Videopreises 2007, Festung Rosenberg, Kronach,
Fürstenbau, September 16–October 21
Come Across, with Gaëlle Boucand, the luggage store,
San Francisco, California, July 13–July 28 (two-person)

2006   *Urban Appearances*, Verein Rosa-Luxembourg-Platz, Berlin,
        Germany, September 26–October 3
        A Satisfied Mind, Pierogi, Leipzig, Germany, July 29–September 2
        Look, Win, Get It On, Art Office, UCLA Department of Art,
        Los Angeles, June 8 (screening)
        European Media Art Festival Osnabrück, Germany, May 10–
        June 18 (screening)
        25th VIPER International Festival for Film, Video, and New
        Media, Kunsthalle Basel, Switzerland, March 16–20 (screening)
        Prix de la Création Vidéo, Videoformes 2006, Clermont-Ferrand,
        France, March 14–18 (screening)

Contributors

Rachel Hooper is associate curator and Cynthia Woods Mitchell Fellow at Blaffer Art Museum. Exhibitions she has organized for Blaffer include *Josephine Meckseper* (2009); *Texas Oil: Landscape of an Industry*, with the Center for Land Use Interpretation (2009); and *Celebutants, Groupies, and Friends: A Photographic Legacy from the Andy Warhol Foundation* (2008).

Christina Linden is the curatorial fellow for 2009–10 at the Center for Curatorial Studies, Bard College. At CCS Bard, she has contributed to projects including *Philippe Parreno* (2010); *At What Moment Does Limestone Become Marble: An Evening Expedition to Kaaterskill Falls*, with Ilana Halperin (2010); and *About the object*, with Amy Patton (2009). She has also worked at galleries, museums, and non-profit art spaces in New York, Berlin, rural Thailand, San Francisco, and Washington, D.C.

Ingo Niermann is a novelist, writer, and editor of the book series Solution. His books include *Solution 186–195: Dubai Democracy* (2010); *Solution 1–10: Umbauland* (2009); *Solution 9: The Great Pyramid*, with Jens Thiel (2008); and *The Curious World of Drugs and Their Friends*, with Adriano Sack (2008). Niermann cofounded the revolutionary collective Redesigndeutschland and invented a universal tomb, the Great Pyramid, proposed for construction in the former East Germany. He currently lives in Berlin.

<table>
<tr><td>

2010 Blaffer Advisory Board

Gordon Goodman, Chair

Emily Baker
Simon Eyles
Stephan Farber
Carol Fleming
Jim Furr
Mark Galicia
Cecily Horton
John Huser
Ann Jackson
Nancy Martin
Andrew McFarland
Sallie Morian
Meg Murray
Judy Nyquist
Sue Porretto
Howard Robinson
John Blaffer Royall
Karen Rozzell
Claudia Schmuckli
Jennifer Smith
Graham B. Snowden
Christine Spin
Lillian Warren

Honorary Member
John Reed
Dr. John Roberts

Lifetime Members
Jane Blaffer Owen †
Jane Dale Owen
Dr. Shirley Rose
Carey C. Shuart
Walter C. Wilson

</td><td>

Blaffer Staff

Claudia Schmuckli
Director and Chief Curator

Jeffrey Bowen
Assistant Director of External
Affairs

Viola Chavez
Assistant Curator of Education

Youngmin Chung
Registrar

Susan Conaway
Director of External Affairs

Rachel Hooper
Associate Curator and
Cynthia Woods Mitchell Fellow

Jonathan Hopson
Museum Preparator

Measa Kuhlers
Chief of Security

James Rosengren
Deputy Director

Katherine Veneman
Curator of Education

Karen Zicterman
Museum Administrator

</td></tr>
</table>

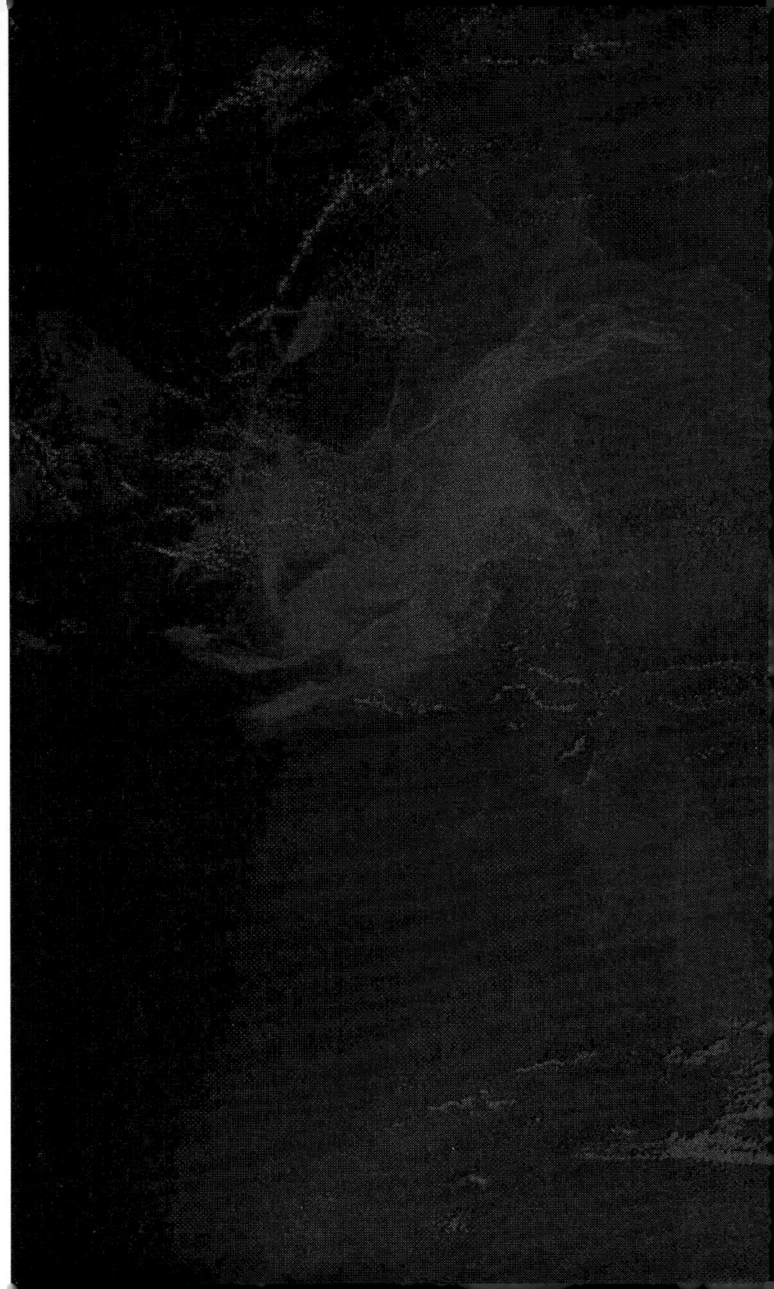